COME, FOLLOW ME

COME, FOLLOW ME

THE COMMANDMENTS
OF JESUS

Invitations to Discipleship

Anthony J. Gittins

Liguori/Triumph
LIGUORI, MISSOURI

Imprimi Potest:
Richard Thibodeau, C.Ss.R.
Provincial, Denver Province
The Redemptorists

Published by Liguori/Triumph
An imprint of Liguori Publications
Liguori, Missouri
www.liguori.org

Library of Congress Cataloging-in-Publication Data

Anthony J. Gittins.
    Come follow me : the commandments of Jesus : invitations to discipleship / Anthony J. Gittins.
       p. cm.
    ISBN 0-7648-1213-0
    1. Christian life—Catholic authors. 2. Jesus Christ—Teachings. I. Title.

BX2350.3.G58 2004
241.5—dc22   2004057652

Printed in the United States of America
07 06 05 04 03 5 4 3 2 1
First edition

Come, Follow Me:
The Commandments of Jesus
is dedicated to the Founders, the Supporters,
and the Beneficiaries of REVIVE.

REVIVE was founded by Peter and Ann-Marie Fell,
Lay Associate Spiritans
(Congregation of the Holy Spirit)
in England.

REVIVE provides welcome, advocacy, and support
for asylum seekers in the North-West of England.

REVIVE aims to offer hope, acceptance,
and the possibility of new life
to people often weighed down by trauma
and uncertainty about the future.

Walking with the lonely and alienated
is sometimes the best we can do.
Believing that God is walking alongside
makes it both appropriate and possible for us.

CONTENTS

INTRODUCTION

We are certainly all familiar, from the *Baltimore Catechism* or the more recent *Catechism of the Catholic Church,* with the Ten Commandments; and no doubt some of us can still recite the commandments of the Church. But who knows about the commandments of Jesus? That is the subject and content of this book.

The Ten Commandments or the Decalogue (remembered by most people as the "Thou Shalt Nots" they grew up with) gave us our first formal understanding of God. They told us, in no uncertain terms, what God expects. They left us with the frightening prospect of what God might do if we were not very careful. The circumstances in which we were taught the Ten Commandments also shaped our idea of what kind of God our God actually is. We surely knew the commandments were not to be trifled with, and we quickly learned the meaning of "grave matter": anything, everything, to do with sex was grave matter. We also established a certain hierarchy in our own minds: apart from the commandments governing sex, some were obviously to be taken more seriously than others. The command not to covet one's neighbor's ox never did seem quite as compelling as the command not to take God's name in vain, and nothing as stringent as the prohibition of murder. But there was always something wrong with this understanding of religion, law, punishment, and God.

In the mid-nineteenth century, A. H. Clough parodied the Ten Commandments with wickedly clever lines like these, exposing the opportunities offered by a strictly literal or legalistic approach:

*No graven images may be
worshiped, except currency.*

*Thou shalt not kill, but needst not strive
officiously to keep alive.*

*Thou shalt not steal; an empty feat,
when it's so lucrative to cheat.*

*Do not commit adultery,
advantage rarely comes of it.*

*Thou shalt not covet, but tradition
approves all forms of competition.*[1]

As commentators have observed, it is very difficult indeed to construct a wholesome and socially responsible way of life on a set of *negative* rules. Many of us know to our cost just how true that is. Sadly, many Christians are not demonstrably wholesome and socially responsible. Many have scarcely grown in moral understanding or fiber since schooldays. And many of us still retain at least traces of a rather dim view of the God of the Old Testament: all wrath and retribution, prohibition and punishment, more concerned with sin than with sympathy, with brimstone than with benevolence, and not noted for intimacy, gentleness, or compassion.

This, of course, is a caricature rather than a portrait: and not even a recognizable one. But many people never did find intimacy with God, and many more left the Church, whether because its ministers were more judgmental than God or because those ministers claimed absolute authority to speak and act on God's behalf. It is a terrible tragedy that so many people have been alienated or estranged from God, often by religion itself.

The commandments of the Church—at least to people like myself—never seemed as absolute or frightening as the Ten Commandments. But they did appear far less important than the Decalogue. Yet they called us to some positive and specific things, and they could have provided a helpful focus for our lives. There used to be six, but the *Catechism of the Catholic Church* has reduced them to five: (1) attending Mass on Sundays and holy days of obligation; (2) confessing once a year; (3) receiving holy Communion during the Easter season; (4) keeping holy the feasts of obligation; and (5) observing fasting and abstinence. To this list is added the duty of contributing to the support of the Church, which many of us remember as the reason the collection plate never passed people by—at least, not without the silent judgment of the person sitting alongside: he or she acted as a social conscience. Not today!

But that was not all the "good Catholic" had to pay attention to: there were other rules—specifically focused on social responsibility as it happens—called the corporal works of mercy. Most people could recite them (feeding the hungry; giving drink to the thirsty; clothing the naked; harboring the stranger; visiting the sick; visiting the imprisoned; burying the dead), whether or not they observed them. And there were spiritual works of mercy, too, though how many of us thought they applied to ourselves is an interesting question in itself (converting the sinner; instructing the ignorant; counseling the doubtful; comforting the sorrowful; bearing wrongs patiently; forgiving injuries; praying for the living and the dead). Thinking of these now evokes another world, another kind of religion even. How many people under sixty can remember them all, or even recognize them now?

So what about the commandments of Jesus? We don't hear much about them, certainly not in the formal or itemized way we learned the Ten Commandments and the others. Yet Jesus pointed to them quite clearly when he said things like: "If you love me, you will keep my commandments" (Jn 14:15). In the same Last Supper Discourse, we find the following: "If you keep my commandments, you will abide in my love (Jn 15:10); "This is my commandment, that you love one another as I have loved you" (Jn 15:12); "You are my friends if you do what I command you" (Jn 15:14); and "I am giving you these commands so that you may love one another" (Jn 15:17), which is even stronger in the *Jerusalem Bible* translation, which is: "What I command you is to love one another."

Jesus also commands us to do some things that, at first sight, seem rather odd: "ask, seek, knock," he says. That is surely not so hard. And these particular commands are actually made easier by the promises that follow: "you *will* receive, you *will* find, the door *will* be opened to you." This is more like an invitation and a guarantee than what we usually think of as a command. But then we don't usually think of love as something to be commanded, although Jesus very deliberately says, "This is *my command to you*: love one another." What could that imply? What might we need to reflect upon?

It seems clear that in recent times people are looking for a better and more intimate understanding of Jesus, both as a historical person and as the Christ of faith. These people have moved beyond the search for a "feel good" Jesus, but perhaps have relatively little familiarity with the Scriptures or with formal theology. Many of them also live in an ambience that does not take too kindly to being told what to do: our culture does not like commands or commandments. Still, many people remain curious about, interested in, or committed to the idea of discipleship.

Looking at the New Testament, it becomes very clear that those who consider themselves disciples—or who aspire to becoming so—are actually commanded by Jesus to behave in a way that will identify them as people who love him, as people who abide in his love, and as people who love "one another" (whatever that might mean). The model for this love, however, is Jesus himself: disciples must love as Jesus loves, and as they are themselves loved. So the "*what?*" question is clear enough; it is the "*how?*" "*who?*" "*where?*" and "*when?*" questions that need further attention. As we look through the words of Jesus for specific commands related to particular situations and persons, we can reasonably deduce that our faithfulness to these will be an appropriate demonstration of our love for God and one another.

With all this in mind, the following pages are offered as a spur to reflection and action. Each takes a particular command of Jesus as its starting point. There are actually far more commands to be found on Jesus' lips than we consider in the following pages. But before we start, a word about the style of this book is in order: about what it attempts to be, and about what it is not.

Exegesis is the recovery of the deepest meanings of a sacred text, by means of critical explanation and the tools of biblical scholarship. This book will certainly look for meanings in the biblical text, but not, primarily, as a scholarly pursuit. Rather, it attempts to bring us face to face with the actual imperatives put on Jesus' lips by one or other evangelist (the "do this" or "do not do that" commands), and to allow ourselves to be challenged by them *in the actual circumstances of our own lives*. We will try not to read things into the text (which would be *eisegesis*), but to allow Jesus' words to challenge our complacency and to evoke in us a more generous response.

Biblical theology, in any or all of its many forms, is essentially a *study* of the Bible. It may focus on the text itself, or on the world behind the text, in order to explain or illustrate by analysis, some truths relating to God and God's designs. This book will stand on the shoulders of biblical theologians, but it is not intended to be a *study* in any formal sense. Rather, it is intended as a form of prayer that may lead us a step closer to our own conversion.

Scholarship is the professional pursuit of an academic discipline. It is often very theoretical, and requires the carefully undertaken and closely reasoned study of a particular topic. This book above all attempts to have a practical bearing on the lives of whoever may read it. That is not to say it does not respect or include a scholarly component, but that focus is not its primary one. It will try to inform and instruct, but explicitly with a view to ongoing conversion and conformity to Christ.

Come, Follow Me: The Commandments of Jesus is simple in concept and simple in execution. Its purpose is to encourage readers in their pursuit of discipleship and to call them to reflect on—and indeed to be appropriately disturbed by—the commandments of Jesus. It is not antiquarian in nature: it does not attempt *only* to identify the original social setting of the commands or the putative intentions of the evangelists. Rather, its purpose is to enhance both our commitment to Jesus (faith) and our pastoral practice (good works). Merely pious devotion to a mythic-historic figure (often a figment of our own imagination or a domesticated and therefore unchallenging pet) is not a measure of authentic discipleship. Nor is mere activism to be identified as faith-filled activity. Rather, we are called, by *Jesus the Christ*—who was born, lived, died, and lives again—to follow his way and live by his lights. This book, like a previous one,[2] is simply an attempt to help renew and refocus our faith-filled discipleship more closely.

The chapters are neither exhaustive nor comprehensive. They are not exhaustive, partly because of my very real and actual limitations, and partly because of my self-imposed limitations: each chapter is of a standard length (a little over two thousand words). The intention is to offer something relatively compact, for meditative prayer rather than for scholarly research. Nor are they comprehensive. I have identified a number of commandments, almost randomly. I have not worked systematically through the New Testament, or even a particular evangelist, picking out every imperative, every command. That would probably be as exhausting as it would be exhaustive. Instead, I offer this book as a kind of companion to the earlier one, *Encountering Jesus*, keeping the length, presentation, and format consistent with that.

Just so that we do not overlook the breadth of Jesus' instructions, we might call to mind some of those commands not dealt with in these pages: go the extra mile; forgive seventy times seventy times; go, and do likewise; take the beam out of your eye; wash each other's feet; repent and believe; do not put God to the test; rejoice and be glad; leave your offering on the altar (and first be reconciled); give to anyone who asks; let your light shine; wipe the dust from your feet; go into the whole world, and so on. So it would not be difficult to choose another set of commandments and present those too.

Finally, these reflections are not presented in any rigorous order. They move between the four evangelists; they deal with a wide range of imperatives; and each one can stand on its own (though an occasional cross reference is provided). Writing them was both a pleasure and a challenge. If reading them is a similar experience, I am gratified. More to the point, however, if they have a positive effect, then God is glorified.

Endnotes

1. Arthur Hugh Clough, "The Latest Decalogue" (1862).
2. Anthony J. Gittins, *Encountering Jesus: How People Come to Faith and Discover Discipleship.* Liguori, Mo.: Liguori/Triumph, 2002.

COME, FOLLOW ME

1

"ASK, AND IT WILL BE GIVEN"

Matthew 7:7

B etween the third and seventh chapters of Matthew's Gospel is a long section the Jerusalem Bible entitled *The Kingdom of Heaven Proclaimed.* The last part of this narrative identifies some characteristics of the true disciple. This is where we find the command: "Ask, and it will be given to you," so it tells us something about discipleship and also something about the kingdom itself. At first sight it seems disarmingly simple-minded; "just ask, and you'll get what you want." This is every child's dream! So there's probably something more to it than that.

The context is an extended discussion on discipleship. Jesus characterizes a true disciple as someone who attempts to respond obediently to whatever he says: in this particular case the disciple is required to *ask.* This is so important that it bears repeating: we are *required* to ask; this is part of the Good News Jesus is proclaiming. Sometimes the Good News feels like a burden that taxes its hearers, and sometimes it is more like a free gift that surprises and delights. Here Jesus is encouraging, inviting, and promising something: "Ask, and you shall receive." Although we have heard these words so often and know them so well, they may still have something new to say to us if we think of them specifically as command, invitation, and promise. But first, here is a story.

Many of us know the almost contradictory saying, "You can't get there from here." We probably judge it to be as apocryphal as it is charming, but I actually heard those words once, while driving in the Irish countryside. I had become hopelessly lost, not three miles from my destination. Coming round a bend in the road, I found the way blocked by several dozen goats—shaggy-haired, multicolored, and twisted-horned—and an old, old farmer, as colorful and shaggy as his herd. Rolling down the window of my car, I asked him for directions. He listened, paused, stroked his chin, and then—with great solemnity and equal certainly—he said: "Well, ye can't get there from here, sir!" Before I could (over)react, he very deliberately and clearly directed me to return the way I had come, and then, after several miles, to head off in a completely different direction!

With goats before me and goats beside me, it seemed imprudent to mumble or object. But it was not even possible to do so, for the farmer shepherded his goats and cleared my way so that I could reverse safely, and then he pointed me in the direction he had indicated. He left me no choice. I still recall looking in the rearview mirror and seeing farmer and flock diminishing as I headed in a direction I had not intended, did not really want to go, and was not at all sure would lead me home.

Now back to the text. Many of us are very self-directed and determined—not to say obstinate—in the way we proceed through life. We are Christians, and we consider ourselves intelligent, responsible, and competent. But perhaps because of that competence and sense of initiative, we do not always respect other people, especially if they appear a little slow. Some of us become self-directed and autonomous and live highly independent lives. There is something deeply wrong with such a spirit of independence, something quite opposed to the true spirit of discipleship.

When Jesus says "ask" (and "seek" and "knock"), he is certainly extending an invitation, but he is doing much more: this really is a command. It is also a universal or general command: it applies to all, to whoever has ears to ear it. It concerns whoever would want to be, or claim to be, a disciple. But, interestingly, it also presupposes that those who obey it are not independent agents but are already related to others, living in a social network or community. This command assumes there is someone nearby, someone *available* to ask, rather than that we are all alone or isolated. Moreover it implies that someone will *respond* positively when we do ask. The problem, of course, is that some would-be disciples are so independent minded that they sometimes stand outside—and perhaps in opposition to—a social network or community. Even if we are actually surrounded by other people, we hesitate to ask for anything; and we might reject the very idea of asking because it bespeaks dependence or *lack* of self-sufficiency. We may need to examine our consciences in this regard, just in case we, too, "can't get *there* from *here.*"

Asking requires a willingness to *acknowledge* our ignorance, or at least it assumes a readiness to rely on someone else. These qualities mark the disciple, but not the self-sufficient individual. Jesus is surely implying that there will come a point of choice in the lives of intelligent, responsible, competent people: they must choose either to cultivate and rely on their own resources, or to admit their need for help. Disciples will know when and how to choose the latter; independent-minded people probably will not.

We all know—and might even be—people like the car-driver who has become hopelessly lost and is getting increasingly frustrated but who absolutely refuses to stop and ask directions. Most typically a male, he will not even concede that he is lost; he blusters and rationalizes rather than asks for help. Now, if we refuse to admit to being lost, it makes no sense to ask directions: we *need not* ask; we *will not* ask; we *cannot* ask! In order to be able to ask, we must first *know* there is something we do not know!

There is more. To be able to receive we must be willing to ask, verbally or by gesture. But, sociologically speaking, the person who asks is in a structurally inferior or dependent position relative to the one who gives (goods, advice, or information). In this sense, a donor is (structurally) superior to a recipient. This is why a person who insists always on giving and *refuses* ever to receive—or to ask— is also refusing to restore the balance between givers and receivers. This idea might be worth pursuing.

It is impossible to imagine a world composed only of givers, for in that world gifts would remain unreceived, and so there would be no gifts at all. It is equally impossible to imagine a world composed only of receivers, for in that world there will be no gifts and no donors. In either case, human interaction is rendered impossible. And if one person insists on only and always being a giver, while another is only and always a receiver, a permanent structural imbalance is created.

Only when there are both givers and receivers, askers and respondents—or, better, when givers are also willing to be receivers and receivers are also able to be givers—can mutuality, reciprocity, and a human community be established. Moreover, the recipient who is unable to *refuse* the gift (because of the constraints of poverty, hunger, or ignorance) will soon come to hate the donor. The ostentatious donor who refuses to accept anything in response or return (not the same as "repayment") is abusing and demeaning the recipients and behaving in a way that actually dehumanizes them. "Foreign aid" sometimes does this to people. So, quite often, does "charity."

Jesus refuses to conform to this pattern: he is highly respectful of other people and their dignity. So when he commands his disciples to ask, he also promises that there will be someone to give what they ask for: he implies that whoever accepts the dependent position of the asker will be appropriately compensated and never demeaned.

Why do so many Christians complain about what they *don't* have, about the lack of orientation in their lives, and about the fact that they don't seem to experience a sense of acceptance or "homecoming" in the faith, when they are so doggedly individualistic that they frequently refuse to ask? Jesus commands, but gently: he does not force anyone. But unless we ask we cannot receive. However, according to Jesus, "everyone who asks [*always*] receives" (Mt 7:8). Do we believe? Do we trust? Have we tried?

Willingness to trust others, to have others trust us, and to negotiate the times in our lives when we *need* to ask—or to respond to those who ask of us—is constitutive of humanness. Therefore it is not altogether surprising that we find this constellation of behaviors visible among the longest-documented people on earth. The Aboriginals of Australia have survived for more than forty thousand years—by asking. Here's how they operate something called "demand sharing." The Australian bush cannot support large numbers of hunter-gatherers, but unless people gather together in groups they cannot survive. The "carrying capacity" of both the (human) band and the (Australian) bush is between thirty and forty people: more than that and the land cannot support them; fewer than that and they cannot survive. Life was always precarious for precontact Aboriginal people, and indeed remains so for contemporary people living far from the towns. "Demand sharing" has developed and has proved to be a lifesaver.

The people in general have very little, and no individual has very much; whatever resources there are must be shared if the group is to survive. There will be times when someone in the group is more needy than others, due to sickness or age, pregnancy or infancy. Then, rather than suffering even more (which would not only be to one's personal disadvantage but to the detriment of the whole group), a person will—and is actually required to—approach someone in the group, and say, in effect: "You'll be happy to lend me a little something!" This signals his or her state of need in simple and unambiguous terms. It is not only the needy person who is required by social convention to make this oblique request: whoever is asked is responsible for responding positively. That might require a "collection" from others in the group, so that whatever is needed, in cash or in kind, can be found. In order to meet the needs of the suffering person, several people will need to contribute and several relationships of indebtedness will be incurred. But the next time there is scarcity, it will be a different person who asks and different people who respond: and the network of give and take, creditors and debtors, will extend until it has embraced everyone in the group. The network will also ensure, as much as possible, the survival of the "un-fittest" and the continuance of the group itself!

This is remarkably close to the idea of a Christian community, but far older than our faith: it has been going on since about forty thousand years *before* Jesus and Christianity! There is surely something we can learn about altruism, vulnerability, trust, and community from the indigenous people of Australia.

It is ironic that the independent-spirited (or selfish) among us so often fail to see how our temperament can militate against discipleship, and how the virtue of graciousness might help us to be more bonded and mutual, more *interdependent* and less independent. Jesus tells us we *should* ask. It is good to ask, and to acknowledge our indebtedness to one another. There is even better news. Jesus promises that those who ask will not be disappointed or humiliated: "Everyone who asks receives" (Mt 7:8). The evangelist uses what is called the Divine passive: the phrase "it will be given" can be translated, "*God* will give." We have God's word for it. We can't lose! Unless, of course, we still refuse to ask.

Some people are reluctant or afraid to ask, because they feel it makes them look stupid. Nothing could be further from the truth. It is often the person who refuses, or fails, to ask who is the truly stupid one. If Jesus commands something, it is certainly not to make us look stupid: perhaps vulnerable, certainly interdependent, but never stupid.

The Irish farmer was, of course, quite right: I could never have gotten "there" from "here." It was entirely necessary to change direction, to find a different way, to experience a tiny conversion. It was his country, after all; and he did know the way! Perhaps as we continue to follow the Way of Jesus, we will be more willing to change direction, perhaps to ask direction, and even to experience a tiny conversion.

～

Prayer

For God's sake, why?
Why do you tell me to ask, Jesus?
You should know what I want.
Can't you just take care of me and do it for me?
What do you expect of me?

I get confused:
About what I want and what I really need,
about what I should ask for
and what I have no business to request.
Asking is so difficult for people like me.

You invited Bartimaeus to ask,
but you trusted him first. Is that the clue?
He asked not for sight, but for vision and insight,
and when he received,
he immediately followed you along the Way.

Help me to ask for what I really need,
for what will make me whole.
Let me believe you trust me, too;
don't let me be afraid to receive.
Don't let me fear to follow.

Questions

1. Would others consider me someone who asks—for information or advice?
2. In my prayer, do I ever ask God (Jesus) directly for help or clarity?
3. Can I get *there* from *here*? If not, what do I need to do?

2

"BE MERCIFUL, JUST AS YOUR FATHER IS MERCIFUL"

Luke 6:36

We all tend to interpret and apply the sayings and teachings of Jesus more or less selectively. There are some words or promises we gladly apply to ourselves ("Blessed are you"). Others though—the so-called "hard sayings"—are less easy to absorb ("Get behind me, Satan"; "Woe to you"). This was true for the contemporaries of Jesus and it remains true for us. The Gospel accounts sometimes tell us that Jesus is speaking to one particular person or to a small group, and that could offer a clue to how his words might (or might not) apply to us individually or collectively. The texts we are considering in these pages have the widest possible application: they are the commandments of Jesus and we need to listen to them in a careful and sober fashion, because they call us to conversion. Here we consider the command: "Be merciful, just as your Father is merciful." Not only is it breathtakingly radical, but those words, "just as your Father is merciful," place us in God's own company!

Context is important here. In Luke's Gospel, immediately after the beatitudes, Jesus delivers both a powerful lesson and a direct challenge to his hearers. The evangelist is careful to identify the fact that Jesus is addressing a great multitude: "a great crowd of his disciples and a great multitude of people from all Judea, Jerusalem, and the coast of Tyre and Sidon" (Lk 6:17). Evidently there is no escape here for any would-be disciples, including ourselves, for Jesus is speaking directly to all those who have ears: to everyone.

In the Gospel of Luke, Jesus addresses people directly with such words as "Blessed are *you*," in contrast to Matthew's account, in which Jesus is more indirect and says, "Blessed are the poor," and so on. But immediately after the people have heard encouragement and promise, the mood changes dramatically. Now Jesus issues some of his most direct and chilling admonitions. The people are warned about their own responsibilities and cautioned not to imagine that God will underwrite their selfishness or complacency. Whoever wants to be numbered among the followers of Jesus—indeed, whoever expects God's blessings—is required not simply to be a grateful recipient of God's goodness but an active agent of God's justice, in and on behalf of the wider community.

Jesus therefore addresses a series of commands directly to everyone. He says, "I say to you that listen…" and then lists four imperatives: "love," "do good," "bless," and "pray for." He exemplifies each, and states the golden rule: "Do to others as you would have them do to you" (Lk 6:31). He then proceeds to explain why anything less than this is simply unacceptable. It is not enough to love people who love us or to be good to those who are good to us. Nor is it sufficient to have reciprocal or mutual arrangements, lending when we fully expect some return. This rather comprehensive catechesis provides a strong profile of the disciple and a rather good job description for contemporary Christians.

So what, concretely, is expected of disciples, of us? It is here that Jesus delivers his radical commands: "Love your enemies," he says; "Do good, expecting nothing in return," he says; "Be merciful," he says: three commands, unequivocal in their meaning and uncompromising in their challenge. Their order and formulation is itself instructive, and each commandment must be obeyed and under-taken by everyone who stands with Jesus; they represent and mirror the way God acts, just as Jesus himself does. Moreover, they build cumulatively—from the simple and specific (though far from easy) command to love one's enemies, via the more open-ended and gen-eral one to undertake whatever is good for another person, to the ultimate expression of love, respect and empathy: mercy toward oth-ers. This is our own focus here, but we need to approach it by stages.

"To err is human; to forgive, divine," said the poet Alexander Pope. To love one's enemies is effectively impossible—even un-imaginable—for almost everyone. It is difficult enough to love our friends (our "loved ones") consistently and purely. But when still reeling from the impact of a savage blow, when incensed at the insult flung in our face, or when utterly devastated by the suffering or even the death of a loved one at the hands of an aggressor, how can we possibly entertain sentiments of love, the ground from which forgiveness grows? When our instinct for self-preservation is stronger than anything except the desire for retaliation or re-venge, how can we possibly find sufficient self-control to be able to entertain feelings of empathy? And when we are so beside our-selves that we can only scream with moral outrage, how could we possibly hear or be attentive to the person of the aggressor, much less acknowledge his or her human dignity or worth? No, at such times, to love one's enemy seems quite impossible, and mercy is unthinkable.

When vindictiveness seems so understandable and hatred is such a natural response, the command to "love your enemies" is utterly outrageous and impossible to fulfill—without divine assis-tance. This brings us to the heart of the matter: Jesus makes de-mands that *are* outrageous by ordinary criteria, yet he also offers to make the impossible possible. Jesus once distinguished between what is humanly impossible, and what—with the help of God—can become possible (Lk 18:27). Evidently we need to turn directly and explicitly to God, the fount and origin of love. Evidently we need a divine boost in order to accomplish what Jesus requires of us. The alternative would be simply to overlook this command.

But if we were to do that, we might live to regret it, and we would certainly fail to become what we are called to be.

"Without me, you can do nothing," Jesus warned; but "ask—and you shall receive," he promised. Destructive retaliation and individual hatred can push society to the brink, as history shows. Only divine invocation and divine intervention have power to restore and heal a broken world. Jesus *commands* his followers to commit themselves to this agenda, while simultaneously offering his help.

The second component of this triple command is this: "Do good [to your enemies], and lend, expecting nothing in return" (Lk 6:35). This again, surely, is too much! How can we do more than acknowledge that it is impossibly ambitious? Jesus was given to articulating the extreme and the impossible (like "tear out your eye," and commands of similar gruesomeness). Yet not only is he quite explicit and consistent on this point, but he seems to be actually raising the social status of enemies to that of one's own compatriots.

The Book of Leviticus refers to fellow countrymen who have fallen on hard times, enjoining that they be treated with authentic hospitality, which means not charging interest, lending money to them freely, and letting them dwell in peace (Lev 25:35–36). This is intended to remind the people of Israel that God treated them in a similar way. But now Jesus goes far beyond even this, indicating that enemies must not simply be tolerated, or even forgiven, but given preferential treatment. It is difficult to imagine what degree of virtue is required if this behavior is to be undertaken. And it is even more surprising and challenging that Jesus is not speaking here to an elite, but to the multitudes, which means that nobody may exempt themselves from his injunctions and still call themselves his followers or disciples! All the more seriously, then, must potential or professional disciples take this command.

Which, finally, brings us to the third of this particular cluster of commands: "Be merciful, just as your Father is merciful" (Lk 6:36). What does this mean, and how does it fit into Luke's thinking? Mercy is one of the most important—indeed it is the cornerstone—of all religious virtues, but its currency has been debased.

Many people today see it either as an optional extra or as somehow *opposed to* justice. This bears thinking about in our own lives. If mercy is truly the cornerstone, then it must be an intentional and practiced part of our lives. We recall among the beatitudes listed by Matthew that Jesus said, "Blessed are the merciful, for they will receive mercy" (Mt 5:7). The Greek word in this text is one from which the English word *alms* directly derives. Luke, however, uses a different word that seems to combine mercy with compassion. If we understand compassion as "suffering with" another person (as opposed to "pity" which can be much more condescending and much less compassionate) that still leaves us to look more closely at mercy itself, for Jesus says we must "be merciful, just as [God] is merciful."

In the technical sense, mercy (*elemosynē* → alms) was understood in Jewish religion as one of the fundamental religious acts. But it was much more than a simple act, like giving a handout to a beggar: it was expected to become an orientation, an attitude, and a way of life. Mercy, or almsgiving in this sense, was sometimes referred to as "a beautiful thing," the epitome of true religion. The Letter of James speaks of true religion as assisting orphans and widows, and remaining unstained by the world (Jas 1:27); this was an example of "a beautiful thing." But there is a much better example—though it is perhaps not as well known.

Of the woman who poured ointment over his feet, Jesus says, "She has done a good deed"—a *New American Bible* (NAB) translation which rather impoverishes it. The *New Revised Standard Version* (NRSV) is better, using the words "she has performed a good service for me"; while the *Amplified Bible* has, "she has done *a good and beautiful thing* to me." Jesus seems to be commending the woman, not simply for doing a good thing, but for doing *the best thing she could possibly have done:* this is mercy at its most concrete. This is more, even, than "a beautiful thing"; it is the most pure religious act. Jesus, we should recall, promised that "wherever the good news is proclaimed in the whole world, *what she has done* will be told in remembrance of her" (Mk 14:9, italics mine). She did a beautiful thing, a work of mercy, and she was explicitly commended by Jesus. Why, then, has she so often been "reduced" to a sinful woman, and then marginalized and her "beautiful thing" effectively forgotten? Jesus said, "Blessed are the merciful, for they will receive mercy," and this woman will undoubtedly receive mercy! The disciples, not surprisingly, do not understand (Mk 14:4–5). The Church in general has not always understood either.

Our final thought is this: we are called not only to be merciful (which is challenging in the extreme), but to be merciful *just as [our] Father is merciful* (Lk 6:36). Rather, we are again commanded to do the impossible! It is God who expresses and embodies mercy. God gives, God does "beautiful things," and God is a God of compassion, empathy, solidarity, and identification with each of us. We are called to be in God's company. We need to reflect on God's mercy to us, and to be converted to *a God's-eye view* of justice: not an eye for an eye, but a preemptive readiness to heal and restore and overwhelm with blessing. Paul's short Letter to Titus says it so very well: "When the goodness and loving kindness of God our Savior appeared, he saved us, not because of any works of righteousness that we had done, but according to his mercy" (3:4–5).

Here we see a contrast between our own attempts at righteousness, and God's righteous and true mercy (*eleos* → alms). No one has said it better than Shakespeare: his soaring poetry is not so much a conclusion as an inspiration for us to "go, and do likewise."

> *The quality of mercy is not strain'd,*
> *It droppeth as the gentle rain from heaven*
> *Upon the place beneath: it is twice bless'd;*
> *It blesseth him who gives and him who takes:*
> *'Tis mightiest in the mightiest; it becomes*
> *The thronèd monarch better than his crown;*
> *His sceptre shows the force of temporal power,*
> *The attribute to awe and majesty,*
> *Wherein doth sit the dread and fear of kings;*
> *But mercy is above this sceptred sway,*
> *It is enthronèd in the hearts of kings,*

It is an attribute to God himself,
And earthly power doth then show likest God's
When mercy seasons justice.[1]

May the justice we live for and live by, always be seasoned with (God's) mercy.

~

PRAYER

God of mercy and compassion,
help us to see with new eyes.
Give us a God's-eye view;
give us a new and unfamiliar perspective.

In times of trouble and sin
we beg you to show us mercy; and so you do.
May we remember this when we are sinned against;
may we grant mercy as mercy has been granted us.

We will never practice the mercy that is yours,
but at least we can remember;
at least, with your help, O God, we can try.

Questions

1. Can I remember a time when I expected God's mercy but was unwilling to show mercy to someone else?
2. Dare I look squarely at the commandment to be merciful *as God is merciful?* Who needs such mercy from me now?
3. "To err is human; to forgive, divine." God has forgiven me; can I not forgive?

Endnotes

1. The Merchant of Venice, Act IV, *i*, 184.

3

"DENY YOURSELVES, TAKE UP YOUR CROSS, FOLLOW ME"

Mark 8:34

An old, faithful, and very tired monk was becoming depressed. Every day was as difficult as the previous one. There seemed to be no end to his tribulations. Why was God so demanding and the cross so heavy? One night Jesus appeared in his dream, called him, and led him down the monastery corridors to an unfamiliar locked room. Opening the door, Jesus invited the old monk to enter and to choose something: anything at all. The old monk entered, and found himself in a storeroom stocked from floor to ceiling with wooden crosses of every imaginable shape and size.

Finally, he thought, God had heard his prayers and was offering a more suitable cross! The monk seized the smallest and lightest, and started to leave, chuckling. But just as he reached the door he stopped, remembering. He remembered who he was and what he had promised. And he was ashamed. Laying down the lightweight cross, he immediately went to the other extreme, found a much heavier one—and was almost crushed under its weight.

Gradually, by trial and error, and by hefting many crosses, he finally found one that felt exactly right. Not as crushing as the heaviest, not as flimsy as the lightest; it was, he felt…appropriate. If only Jesus had asked him to carry this, and not the deadweight he had been dragging for so long!

Jesus was waiting outside the door. The monk thanked him heartily, and prepared to carry his newfound cross. Jesus, smiling, asked him to lay it down and look at it more closely. Then the old monk saw the writing: a name. Going down on one knee, because his eyes were dim, he was able to make out—his own name! Bringing himself to his feet, he heard Jesus say: "Why did you not trust me, just a little longer? I picked this cross for you. I knew what you could carry. This *is* the cross you have been carrying all these years: your cross, and mine." The old monk was embarrassed, but encouraged, too. He returned to his cell, slept soundly, and woke very early, with renewed strength and purpose.

The command we consider now will test our faithfulness and trust. Jesus commanded disciples to ask, seek, and knock; and they (and we) could look at each commandment separately. By contrast, the three identified here—deny yourself, take up your cross, follow me—are so connected as to be inseparable. The monk's story makes the point quite well: we must deny ourselves *in order* to turn our attention to the cross; we take up our cross *as a way* of following Jesus; and followers of Jesus proceed *by way of the cross.* The components fit together.

"Self-denial" is almost a cottage industry these days: first, people eat or drink excessively, and then they work out excessively (chanting "no pain, no gain"). Even some Christians wait for Lent or Advent, willing to embrace "self-denial" *as a way to lose weight, save money, cleanse the system,* and so on. But this is only self-indulgence in disguise. Sadly, religious discipline can easily become a means to a selfish end, used to impress others, and even ourselves, without involving conversion at all. What Jesus asks is very different: the denial of the ego, of the selfishness and self-centeredness that marks our lives. (Even that is not an adequate statement, for the denial of the ego must really be for the sake of the kingdom, the realm, the community, the poor: for God and others.) True denial of self serves solidarity or interdependence, not individualism or independence.

Even delayed or deferred gratification is not authentic self-denial in the spirit of Jesus (though perhaps a step in that direction), for we are called to deny certain kinds of gratification completely. Yet this is not the "holy masochism" or self-inflicted misery that many of us are familiar with. Jesus calls his disciples to a new way of being community, a new way of visualizing the world: to a social reality marked by redistribution, equity, empathy, and generosity of spirit. It would be a kind of utopia, in the sense that it mirrors God's own idea of the way the world should be, when the poor experience God's preferential option mediated through their neighbors, and where self-interest yields to the imperative of the well-being of each and all.

"Deny yourself," says Jesus to those with ears and those capable of making choices. It directly challenged his own society, whose main currency was honor and whose main fear was shame. True self-denial will privilege others and honor God. The commandment of Jesus not only strikes at the selfishness in his own culture but at the sin in our own.

Before we have had time to internalize this first command, the second follows: "take up your cross." There is no sentimentality here, but quite possibly scandal. No one would willingly have taken up a cross (or crossbeam): only condemned people did that, and only because it was *imposed* on them as the preliminary to their execution. It actualized the death sentence. Jesus is asking something outrageous by civilized standards. But he is not finished: "and follow me," he says. Follow, not by way of a pleasant stroll in congenial company, but follow the one weighed down by a crossbeam! Under that weight, no one could walk in a straight line or for any real distance, yet Jesus expects his followers to have extraordinary discipline, strength, and clear-sightedness: "deny yourself, take up your cross, and follow me!"

Either this makes no sense at all (and each element is more
bizarre and outrageous than the previous one), or it makes deeply
intuitive sense (each element building into the next with compelling logic). But however intuitively we might grasp the inner logic,
the triple command can never be *easy* to implement (though, almost forestalling our objections, Jesus did say, "my yoke is easy,
and my burden is light" [Mt 11:30]). The real question for us is
not whether it is easy but whether it is possible.

Everything will depend on the last phrase, "follow me." This
provides the focus and encouragement to "take up your cross";
"take up your cross" gives purpose to the command to "deny yourself." But the problem here is enormous. It is what we know as the
scandal of the Gospel, the *scandal* of Jesus, and the *scandal* of the
cross. How can we follow one who was charged as a criminal and
whose death was the most shameful of all: death by crucifixion?

We use *scandal* in two apparently different ways. On the one
hand, it is something to be avoided at all costs. Jesus regarded scandal as possibly the worst kind of evil, and reserved some of his
most uncompromising words for anyone who should scandalize
one of the "little ones" (Mt 18:5–6), and leaving us with the grue-
some image of someone who should pluck out an eye rather than
be scandalized (Mt 5:29; 18:9). And Paul emphasizes that believers
must "not...do anything that makes your brother or sister stumble"
(Rom 14:21). Here, scandal has the meaning of "causing to sin."

On the other hand, Jesus himself is perceived as a scandal, and
Saint Paul both acknowledges and exploits this, calling would-be
followers to embrace this scandal as passionately as they embrace
life itself. Technically, it is not Jesus himself but his cross that is the
scandal to many. In his day, everyone knew the meaning of a cross,
and no sane person would risk the capital punishment it signified. A
cross against the horizon was the clear mark of a criminal, someone
who had been himself seduced or led astray ("scandalized") by evil.

The word *scandal* shares its etymological history with other
words containing the same initial double consonant: words like
scan (meaning *to examine* verse; and *ascend* or *descend* [from the

Latin *scandere,* which retains the "*sc*" sound], meaning *to climb up or down.* A *scandal,* in addition to its common meaning of a stumbling block or trap, refers to something prominent or visible, something to be examined carefully, *because it is potentially painful.* This is a helpful perspective, as we examine just how Jesus and the cross constitute a scandal, and how much pain it entails, not only for Jesus but for those who follow and take up their own crosses. The crucifixion of Jesus is offensive enough in itself, but actually to *proclaim* the crucified one as the Christ, God's anointed, the promised Messiah—that is unquestionably a scandal, and painful for both the Jews [who demand signs] and for the Greeks [who desire wisdom].[1] Where can there possibly be a Divine sign or godly wisdom here?

The Way of Jesus, the righteous one, would—paradoxically—converge with the way of the cross. The Holy One of God would be crucified as a criminal and as a warning to others. His example, therefore, was to be avoided at all costs...unless: unless he *remained* the Holy One of God and his crucifixion was an obscenity and a travesty of God's justice!

Those who follow Jesus embrace the "folly" of the cross because, despite the odium of the cross itself, they see that following Jesus is the righteous thing to do. Being crucified (whether for Jesus or for the disciple) makes no apparent sense, but being righteous makes all the sense in the world. So disciples put commitment to God's righteousness ahead of vindication by the world. Even more, they want to continue following Jesus, both because Jesus leads the way and because they believe his words.

Saint Paul argues that the cross stands as the meeting or the parting of the ways. Those who follow Jesus will reach their destination as he did: by way of the cross. Most people follow the way of conventional wisdom. But for those who remain faithful to Jesus, "conventional wisdom in the light of the Gospel becomes foolishness."[2] The opposite is also true: in the light of conventional wisdom, the Gospel is foolishness. So people must choose. The only possible way for us to commit ourselves to the "scandal" of the

cross—to take up our cross—is if we can say with Peter, "You are
the Messiah [the Christ], the Son of the living God" (Mt 16:16).
Otherwise it is only and always a stumbling block (rather than
something prominent, to be carefully examined); as such, it will
always give offense to pious ears and eyes.

In 1909 Ernest Shackleton came within seventy-five miles of
the South Pole, but was forced to make the bitter yet wise decision
to give up. Less than five years later he placed the following advertisement in a newspaper:[3]

> Men wanted for hazardous journey. Small wages, bitter cold,
> long months of complete darkness, constant danger, safe
> return doubtful. Honor and recognition in case of success.

Five thousand people replied, including many women; and in
1914 a second expedition set sail in the ill-fated ship, *Endurance*.

Endurance was caught, and slowly crushed, in the pack ice, not
far from the Pole. Shackleton placed safety first: the mission was in
service of humanity and scientific knowledge and he refused to
sacrifice his expeditionary force needlessly. But there was dissent
over his decision to seek safety by abandoning the Pole a second
time. There was also fear. Demanding unqualified obedience,
Shackleton vowed that he would save all hands. Team goals were
identified, whereupon the leader stated that he would tolerate
no dissent. He asserted his leadership with great moral force
and with the authority of a commander. He also favored his
weakest men, slept in the same tent as the most difficult, gave
the precious reindeer-skin sleeping bags to others, and maintained morale by talking with everyone, especially the surly,
the antisocial, and the fearful. He succeeded in sustaining morale, gaining the loyalty and following of all, and, after an epic
journey, did indeed reach South America and thence Europe
without losing a single man!

"Follow me," says Jesus. He also promised that none of those
who followed him would be lost.[4]

Those who volunteered and those who actually followed Ernest Shackleton, were not looking for cheap thrills, anymore than were the hundreds who volunteered as firefighters immediately after 9/11; only months later, more than three hundred new firefighters graduated, passionate to fill the shoes of those who had died. The world we live in now has no real shortage of heroes, only the shortage of a cause to live for and to die for. But, perhaps, we also suffer from a crisis of imagination. People with imagination constantly ask, "What if?" and "Why not?"—until they discover something unusual, even close to impossible, but eminently worthwhile.

Jesus commands nothing that he does not also underwrite. What if we were to hear this triple command as if for the first time: "Deny yourself, take up your cross, follow me"? There are all manner of rational objections and problems. But that never deterred the Shackletons of this world, and such leaders never lack for followers. Why do I not take Jesus as seriously as he takes me? What am I waiting for?

~

PRAYER

"Life, liberty, the pursuit of happiness";
these are inscribed in stone.
"Deny, take your cross, and follow";
these are inscribed in flesh.

Hearts of stone—or hearts of flesh?
Rights—or duty?
Why does it profit if we gain everything,
only to lose it all?

Lord, sometimes you can be so demanding;
and sometimes you are impossible.
But you help make the impossible possible,
and you can help us desire denial.

Questions

1. Is my cross tolerable? Do I trust God?
2. What is the quality of my self-denial?
3. Do I want to be a hero, or to follow the way of Jesus?

Endnotes

1. See 1 Cor 1:18–25.
2. Mary Ann Getty, *1 Corinthians*. In the *Collegeville Bible Commentary: New Testament*. Robert Karris (ed.). Collegeville, Minn.: The Liturgical Press, 1992, 1108.
3. This advertisement is justly famous, but these may not be the exact words. Some people maintain it is a legend.
4. Except Judas, we may think. In John's Gospel (17:12) Jesus says that not one was lost except "the one destined to be lost"—a translation of "the son of perdition." There has been an almost universal identification of Judas as this person. Yet Jesus also maintained his constant care and love. Jean Daniélou suggested that "the Son of Perdition" is more likely to be Satan, who seduced Judas (Jn 13:2). See Francis J. Moloney, *The Gospel of John*. Collegeville, Minn.: Michael Glazier/Liturgical Press, 1998, 470.

4

"DO NOT FEAR, ONLY BELIEVE"

Mark 5:36

T his command, repeated so often and in so many different contexts and forms, encapsulates one of the central principles of the philosophy (and indeed the theology) of Jesus: fear must be supplanted, and faith must be firmly planted in its place. Fear, which can sometimes be constructive (as part of our "fight or flight" reflex) and can play a part in self-preservation, can also become destructive by paralyzing and controlling us, preventing our living as free agents and mature human persons. This is what Jesus is addressing here. And since his words are formulated specifically as a command, we should perhaps begin by looking carefully at the force that the imperative form gives them.

Jesus is not making a suggestion or even a recommendation. Nor is he offering gentle encouragement here. He quite deliberately uses the imperative mood. Moreover, what he says is very pointedly constructed in the form of a pair of commands. In the Markan version, they stand in apposition to each other. That is to say, they need to be taken together, because each one throws light on the other. Their particular context also offers us some enlightenment about their urgency and application. So, after we explore

the context of these commands, we can proceed to recontextualize
them in order to apply them appropriately to the actuality of our
own lives.

In Mark's narrative, Jesus has just come from the country of
the Gerasenes. Most of those who listened to Jesus would have nothing good to say for the Gerasenes: they were foreigners and pa-
gans. But Jesus' hearers were going to be surprised! Having healed
a deeply troubled man in Gerasene country, Jesus then commissioned him to be a healing evangelizer in his turn (Mk 5:19–20).
That episode concluded with the observation: "Everyone was
amazed." Not surprisingly!

Now, as the present story continues to unfold, we are on the
other side of the lake where Jesus is about to have a double encounter: first with Jairus, a synagogue official whose daughter is
gravely ill, and then with an unnamed woman who is literally bleeding to death (Mk 5:21–43). At the end of the story, when the woman
has been cured and Jairus' daughter has been raised to life, the
words that concluded the Gerasene passage reecho very clearly as
Mark says: "They were overcome with amazement" (Mk 5:42).
Then, immediately after this passage, when Jesus encounters some
hostility directed at himself, Mark uses the verb again, this time
applied to Jesus: "He was amazed at their unbelief" (Mk 6:6). In
close succession we have three "amazing" encounters or observa-
tions about reactions to encounters with Jesus. This, then, forms
the context into which the command, "Do not be afraid, only believe" must be placed if we are to grasp its full significance. Perhaps, if we ponder these events, we too will be suitably amazed.

The persistence of the hemorrhaging woman—who, significantly, had "heard" (Mk 5:27) about Jesus and then comes to him
in response to reports about his godly works—will elicit the gentle
and affirming response: "Daughter, your *faith* has made you well"
(Mk 5:34, italics mine). Anthropologists and other scholars tell us
that in the culture of ancient Israel, a major criterion of humanness was "having ears." This implied the capacity to hear, to internalize, to understand, and to respond in an appropriate way. It is

therefore not at all insignificant that this woman (effectively excluded from human society by virtue of her gender and her affliction) is identified as someone who had *heard* about Jesus and responded accordingly. We recall how often Jesus berated people for having ears yet not hearing, or appearing to be human but actually having closed ears (Mt 13:14, Lk 6:46–49). Jesus had identified his kin, his *true* mother and siblings, as "those who *hear* the word of God and do it" (Lk 8:21, italics mine).

At this point, the *dénouement* of the story about the synagogue leader's daughter takes place. Jesus had followed the synagogue leader,[1] indicating that he would do something to help the man and his daughter. But just after he had attended to, and commended the faith of, the bleeding woman, some people arrived with bad news for the sick girl's father: "Your daughter is dead" (Mk 5:35). It is as stark, unequivocal, and final a statement as it can possibly be.

The text says that Jesus *overheard* this remark. In an interesting play on words, Mark will demonstrate just how human Jesus is: he listens, he *hears*, he acts: blessed indeed are those who have ears! The question is: will the synagogue official be among those assured of blessedness?

Jesus immediately turns to the man and utters the command we are considering here: "Do not fear, only believe" (Mk 5:36). The man has just heard the brutal news of his young daughter's death and has hardly had time to take it in, yet he is being told not to be afraid, not to worry! It is almost as if Jesus anticipates the man's fear; he is issuing a preemptive command. If so, then, he has a very good grasp of the experience of those around him. But two things are very significant about this account. First, it was actually the official who had approached Jesus, fallen at his feet, and requested that he come and save his daughter's life; so this man had *already* shown signs of faith. And second, the last words that had been on the lips of Jesus had been spoken in commendation of the faith of a woman crippled by an affliction that had marked her for twelve years. So now the stage is set for testing the synagogue official's faith.

Mark keeps his readers in suspense, as he has Jesus—along with a select group of disciples and the girl's father—move off toward the house. When Mark tells us that the daughter was twelve years old, we immediately make the connection with the twelve years' affliction of the older woman. After twelve years of unrelenting illness and victimization, the older woman's life has become so marginal as to be effectively over. By contrast, having only lived for twelve years, the younger woman—still hardly more than a girl, and only on the verge of her adult life—is already dead. Jesus is about to restore life to each, and the synagogue leader will be the bridge between each of these lives.

The NRSV translates the words of Jesus as "do not *fear*, only believe," while other translations say "do not *be afraid*, only believe." It may be helpful to ponder the nuances here. The phrase "do not be afraid" seems to address an actual state of being (*being* afraid), while "do not fear" identifies a more transitory emotion (*fear*).

The actual state of being afraid—or chronically agitated, ill at ease, or simply not at peace—seems to be a malaise of our own times; many people go through life like that, in a permanent state of unease or dis-ease. One of the last things Jesus did, we remember, was to leave his disciples with his gift of peace, "a peace the world cannot give." Up to that point, he had repeatedly told them not to be afraid. It has been said that the phrase, "Do not be afraid," occurs 365 times in the Bible—one for each day of the year! In the account we are considering here, Jesus seems to be encouraging people and enabling them *not to live in a state of fear*. So, "do not *be afraid*" rings truer, and is more convincing and encouraging, than a simple "do not fear."

Likewise, we may distinguish between "believe" and "have faith." Most translations have "believe," but the *New American Bible* uses the words "just have faith." Most of us may take it for granted that religions are always concerned with matters of belief, systems of belief, and the adherence to a set of "beliefs." This is a rather narrow view, however; many of the world's religious systems are not primarily characterized by "beliefs" at all, but by "praxis" or appropriate behaviors. More importantly, there is a fundamental difference between adhering to *beliefs* and having *faith.*

Faith bespeaks *relationship,* and Christianity calls us not simply to believe in propositions, or to hold certain beliefs about God, but actually to have a developing relationship with God. This is precisely what authentic faith entails: *a developing relationship— with God.* One of the saddest facts about religion is that it may succeed in instilling a set of beliefs (such as those systematized in any catechism) but without ever bringing a person to faith. Many of us are in fact more familiar with *religious instruction* than with *faith formation.* But the former without the latter will not produce truly faith-filled people, people with a developing relationship with Jesus and with God. This is why it seems preferable for us to hear these words of Jesus as both command and invitation: "Do not be afraid, only have faith." It is time we took those words seriously; the one who speaks them is the one with power to make them a reality.

Our common Jewish-Christian tradition is—uniquely among the world's religions—based on the notion that it is not only possible but desirable that people should have a developing relationship with God. This is an amazing claim. Jesus was constantly referring to his own relationship with his *abba* as the foundation of his life and ministry. Yet many Christians are "believers" but not necessarily "people of faith." They do not *know God* intimately, however much they may *know about* God. For such people—and indeed for all of us at times—these words of Jesus need to be heard and taken to heart: "only have faith." We *can* know God, and we *should* know God—in an ongoing, developing way; this is the promise and fruit of our Christian faith.

Jesus says quite clearly that it is not those who believe (those who say "Lord, Lord") who will enter the kingdom of God, but those who have faith: those who do the will of God because they are attentive to the inspiration of God in their daily lives. We cannot possibly expect to know *in advance* what is demanded of us, since our lives consist of so many new and never-before-experienced

situations and occurrences. Only if we are coming to have the mind
of God will we be attentive to the moods and the moments in a
faith-filled and fearless way. Only if we have an intimate, developing understanding of how to be more godly as our lives unfold will
we be able to stand among the true disciples, those who follow
Jesus. The prayer of Saint Richard of Chichester says it very well:

> *O Lord, three things I pray:*
> *To see thee more clearly,*
> *To love thee more dearly,*
> *To follow thee more nearly,*
> *Day by day.*

That is the prayer of the disciple with eyes fixed on Jesus; not
looking down, not filled with fear, but alive with the promise and
filled with the faith. It could be our own prayer, especially when
we sense how fragile is our faith. Jesus was "amazed" at the lack of
faith of those who were actually witnesses to miracles and yet not
liberated from their own crippling fear. And yet the "possessed"
Gerasene man had been liberated from fear, and called and commissioned by Jesus to proclaim the good news in the cities of the
Decapolis (Mk 5:18–20). No wonder people were amazed. The
wonder is that many of us lack the imagination to be amazed by
what Jesus can do by calling and commissioning us—once we no
longer fear; once we only believe.

Saint Richard's prayer might also take us back to the story of
the woman who *overcame fear* and *already believed*—even before
she was healed. True, she came to Jesus "in fear and trembling,"
but that was largely because she was suddenly on the public stage.
She only got to be on the public stage in the first place, *because of
her faith*. Jesus said it explicitly: "Daughter, your faith has made
you well" (Mk 5:34). Truly, it is not miracles that make faith, but
faith that makes miracles.

~

Prayer

God of encouragement, God of invitation,
you are always reaching out
and reaching into our lives
with your word and sacrament.

Jesus, who is your living word,
speaks your own words:
"Do not fear; only have faith."

Give us ears to hear and hearts to embrace.
Give us the capacity to move beyond our fears
to where your freedom reigns.

God, give us the faith we need,
in order to move the mountains
that block the landscape
and obscure the view of your reign.

Questions

1. If faith moves mountains, do I live by my religious belief(s) or by my faith in God?
2. Jesus gives the gift of peace; the world cannot give it. Do I want it? Do I ask?
3. Do I have a developing relationship with God? What am I doing about it?

Endnotes

1. In itself, this is interesting and unusual. Jesus usually calls and other people follow. Here he is showing his attentiveness to another's needs.

5

"Do Not Work for the Food That Perishes"

John 6:27

F ood is basic, a staple, and not only for sustaining bodily life; it is also a basic metaphor (particularly in the Gospels of Mark and John) for talking about life beyond the purely physical level. The *metaphor* of food is used in the New Testament when people's priorities or deep values are under scrutiny.

Let us examine the Gospel of Mark for the use of this metaphor. Several threads run right through it such as *the Way* of Jesus, or his commitment to the journey to Jerusalem and death. One thread concerns food and, if we traced it carefully, we would notice a striking pattern and a theme that is absolutely central to Mark's purposes. He repeatedly uses the Greek word *artos*, which translates as the English word *bread*.

We might be very surprised and illuminated if we identified every occurrence of *artos* in this Gospel. But in order to understand the theme more clearly, it might be helpful to ask some focal questions: Where is the *artos* to be found? Who has it? Who does not? Who is searching for it? Who is not? Who provides it? How is it to be found? What is its purpose and its nourishing power? (In short, what *exactly* is it?) What happens to those who lack *artos*? The more we add to these questions, the better we can understand the "food" Jesus is talking about, the food he wants to offer for our nourishment and our life.

Anyone who reads through Mark's Gospel, simply following the trail of *artos* laid down by its author, will discover a great deal about faithful discipleship: who are the authentic disciples, who are the merely curious, and who are the "resisters", the uncomprehending, or the unconcerned. Anyone who pursues this process will gather a comprehensive understanding of discipleship itself, and of how it applies to the context of his or her own life. If we do this ourselves, we may find we can identify other questions and challenges for our own faithfulness to Jesus. Am I seriously seeking the *artos* of life? Do I know where to look? Am I looking in the right place? Am I being nurtured by the *artos* Jesus offers? What else do I need to do in order to find, to grasp, to eat, and to be nourished by the *artos*? Do I remain hungry for *artos*—or have I become sated, or bloated, or perhaps I have even lost my appetite? These questions are food for thinking and food for acting: they may stimulate our faith-buds.

The specific commandment we are looking at here is not actually from Mark's Gospel but from John's. The *artos*—or bread—theme that is elaborated in Mark certainly provides us with an approach, but the Johannine context provides a particularly helpful setting for a reflection on discipleship. Then we can combine the commandment as articulated in John's Gospel and the insights about bread (*artos*) in Mark's Gospel.

In John's Gospel, as we recall, the whole of Chapter Six is devoted to what is called "The Bread of Life Discourse." It begins with an account of the feeding of the five thousand; and John states quite pointedly that Jesus knew exactly what he was going to do, that he ordered the disciples carefully to collect the leftover pieces, and that there was enough to fill twelve baskets, symbolic of the twelve tribes of Israel and indicating that Jesus was perfectly able to feed "everyone." But the evangelist now wants to demonstrate that the so-called "disciples" were far from the kind of disciples Jesus was looking for, and that they had virtually no understanding of what Jesus was about. So he follows the feeding of the multitude with the story of the storm on the lake, the walking on the water, and the disciples' terror.

It is helpful, in view of the way I want to pursue this reflection, to turn back to Mark's account at this point. Mark (chronologically the first evangelist) tells the story of the storm on the lake and the walking on the water. He, too, places it immediately after the feeding of the multitude. But this is how he concludes his account: "[Jesus] got into the boat with them and the wind ceased. And they were utterly astounded, for they did not understand about the loaves [= *artos*], but their hearts were hardened" (Mk 6:51–52). Here is food for thought.

Now it is the next day, and John tells us that the crowd, having attempted to find and reach Jesus, was addressed by words that are solemn but perhaps also rather reproachful: "You are looking for me, not because you saw signs, but because you ate your fill of the loaves. Do not work for the food that perishes, but for the food that endures for eternal life, which the Son of Man will give you" (Jn 6:26–27).

Now we can connect these words of Jesus and the bread (*artos*) theme of Mark. Jesus is calling people to deeper insight and understanding, to deeper faith, and to a reflection about what really sustains life and makes it possible and meaningful, apart from what is very obvious and literal: food, or bread.

Many of us live in a culture of abundance. Some, as we say, do not so much eat to live as live to eat: we overeat and we grow obese (at an alarmingly increasing rate and a dangerously younger and younger age). At the very same time, billion-dollar industries have been generated, designed to feed our insatiable appetites without making us fat: anything seems preferable to encouraging a different way of living! Some people seek food that is downright unhealthy, while others look for faux-food, food that simply titillates.

This combines greed and lack of self-control[1] in a potentially lethal mixture.

As disciples, we might reflect on our own attitude to food in general, to actual physical food: Are we addicted or in control? Do we strive to eat healthily and to exercise accordingly? And so on. Then, looking more metaphorically at the food that sustains us: What is our food of choice? What do we live for, crave, or depend on? Is it fame or flattery, power or possessions or popularity, or simply more of everything? "Where your heart is, there is your treasure," said Jesus. Here is more food for thought.

There is something sad, pathetic even, in the posturing of one who aspires to be a Christian and yet is so committed to chasing fame or money, prosperity or reputation, that there is no time for anything else. Essential components of any would-be Christian are a social conscience and a commitment to the service of others. When Jesus fed the multitude, he included *everyone,* and there was enough food for all. Significantly, there were even leftovers that could be gathered and redistributed. Christians are called to be disciples and to follow the example of Jesus. This is precisely why Jesus commands his own disciples to examine their priorities, to see if their actions belie their claims to be true disciples. It is why he urges them to focus on what he identifies as the priority: not the "food" that perishes—whether fame or fortune, power or possessions—but the "food" that endures to eternal life.

It is relatively easy to *say* that we are, or want to be, disciples. It is not very difficult to say "Lord, Lord." But that simply is not enough. Only those who are committed to doing the will of God are true and authentic disciples. It is so easy to delude ourselves, to begin to believe we are what we claim to be. But the urgent and insistent reminder of Jesus will not be silenced. We may not hear it; we may turn up the volume of our lives; but the command remains: "Do not labor for the food that perishes."

Joan Chittister once asked: "What do you want to be caught dead doing?" It is not a facetious question; it is the most important question of our lives. If we know what we would like to be caught dead doing we have some focus, some priority. If we know what we would like to be caught dead doing we have something to live for. But if we are true Christians or truly Christian, what *we* would like to be caught dead doing ought to be just about what nobody else would want to be caught dead doing! That is because we are supposed to be countercultural in the sense of not allowing ourselves to be seduced by the priorities of the surrounding culture. Those priorities—and the excess to which they lead—include, of course, many varieties of "food," from groceries or victuals to greed or acquisitiveness, and extending to all kinds of self-indulgence: we do not need a list. What we may need is a simple reminder: where our heart is, there our treasure is. In other words, "do not labor for the food that perishes, but for the food that endures"— the food that becomes the treasure that opens us to the kingdom, the realm of God.

What and where is the nonperishable and enduring food? Immediately after commanding his disciples to labor for this food, Jesus actually offers to give it to them! The complete verse of John's Gospel reads, "Do not work for the food that perishes, but for the food that endures for eternal life, *which the Son of man will give you*" (Jn 6:27, italics mine). As an aid to further reflection, here are three points.

The first point concerns Jesus' own promise: it is immediate, free, and comprehensive, without limits or conditions. Jesus himself makes no stipulations; it is the disciples who ask, "What must we do?" (Jn 6:28), whereupon Jesus calls them to believe (Jn 6:29). The Greek verb "to believe" sometimes means "to believe [someone]" or "to believe in [someone]"; it can also mean "to believe about [someone or something]" or "to believe [that something is the case]." Here, Jesus is calling disciples to believe *him*, to believe *in him*, and not simply to believe certain things about him or to accept what other people say about him. This is unequivocally a call to personal faith, to a relationship. We already noted that the great novelty of our faith is the idea that believers can have—indeed are called to have—*a developing relationship with God.*[2] Here Jesus explicitly extends that invitation! Here is even more food for thought.

The second point is this: Jesus discloses his own focus and motivation by identifying his relationship with his *abba*. Already the author of John's Gospel has shown how Jesus used the image of food, and how little his would-be disciples understood. They returned from buying their own food, having missed the encounter between Jesus and the Samaritan woman at the well. John's Gospel picks up the story: "Meanwhile the disciples were urging him [Jesus], 'Rabbi, eat something.' But he said to them, 'I have food to eat that you do not know about.'…Jesus said to them, 'My food is to do the will of him who sent me and to complete his work'" (Jn 4:31–32, 34). This is what Jesus will later elaborate: that as he is sustained by doing God's will, so they will be sustained by believing him, which means staying close to him, learning from him, and going as he commissions them, to complete his work as he completes his Father's. *This* is the food that endures for eternal life. *This* is the food that Jesus gives his disciples.

The third point simply elaborates the first two. Having called his disciples and promised them what they need, Jesus explains what his own "food" is, and how it must become theirs. We know that the disciples are slow to hear and slow to learn, so when Jesus rephrases his message, it should be encouraging for them and for us. It operates on two levels, one straightforward and the other coded. "I am the bread of Life," he says (Jn 6:48). So they need not look very far; Jesus is right there among them. This statement could not be clearer, though it will take them a very long time to understand. But it is also a coded message: here is an "I AM" (or *ego eimi*, Greek for *I am*) statement. Yahweh was revealed to Moses as "I Am Who Am," and whenever the evangelists want to show Jesus identifying himself most intimately with God, they put this phrase on his lips. So here Jesus is disclosing his most intimate identity. Even if the first disciples did not yet grasp the full meaning of what he said, the later disciples—ourselves—certainly should. "I am the bread of life." Now we know: we should not work for the food (*artos*) that perishes; and Jesus himself is the *artos* of life. Here is a final, nourishing, portion of food for thought.

~

PRAYER

*It's important that we ask
if we're heading the right way.
Jesus is calling.*

*We must not labor for bread
that fails to nourish.
Otherwise we'll starve.*

*Jesus says "Only look for me,
follow me: I AM
the WAY, the TRUTH and the LIFE."*

Questions

1. How would I identify the (actual and metaphorical) food I work for?
2. Where is the hunger and the thirst in my life, currently?
3. What do I want to be caught dead doing?
4. What likelihood is there that I might think differently and be converted?

Endnotes

1. Self-control is part of the command, "Deny Yourself, Take Up Your Cross, Follow Me." See Chapter 3.
2. For the idea of a developing relationship with God, see Chapter 4, "Do Not Fear, Only Believe."

6

"Do Not Worry About What You Are to Say"

Mark 13:11

ost people, reasonably enough perhaps, try to organize and control their lives as much as possible: they do not like to leave too many things to chance. The dominant cultures in which many of us live not only foster a spirit of control and independence but also make it difficult for us to relax, to trust, and to share. Yet none of us is immortal and none of us can completely control the world we live in. Worry or fear still seems to stalk us or to lie in wait for us at some time or another. Life is not always easy. Even organized lives are not worry-free.

In many ways, the world of Jesus and his contemporaries was considerably more difficult for people to control than our own. They may have made a virtue out of a necessity by learning to operate more corporately or communally than some of us can. Still, in the pages of the New Testament we often encounter Jesus encouraging people not to be afraid—which only serves to indicate that, even with friends to rely on, they *were* afraid. But Jesus is no naive optimist: he wants to make it possible for people not to be plagued by chronic worry or paralyzed by fear. Jesus wants to offer his own strength, courage and power.

"Do not be afraid, only have faith." Jesus said this, or something very much like it, on many occasions. The First Letter of John tells us that "perfect love casts out fear" (4:18), but none of us, including the original disciples, can claim to have such love. Fear is clearly not far away, and on many occasions it dominates their lives and our own. The disciples were afraid when Jesus came walking on the water in the storm (Mt 14:26), and afraid when Jesus was transfigured (Mt 17:7). So what kinds of things are people afraid of, and why is it so necessary to transcend fear in order to come to mature discipleship?

Not unsurprisingly, people fear what they do not know, cannot control, or believe to be intimidating or likely to produce failure. Such fears are partly instinctive, acting as a primitive "early warning system" of impending danger, and thus designed for self-preservation. Other fears are released when people know that they face something they cannot avoid, but they sense they have neither the experience nor the capacity to deal with it. Fear of personal failure is often intensified when people know that their social standing may be negatively affected if they are seen to fail: other people's opinions *do* count.

Worry, or anxiety, is a form of fear, but is often generated not by what actually challenges or threatens, so much as by our anticipation of what *might* happen but has not yet happened. In fact it might never happen, and for reasons that may be completely beyond our control; yet we worry about negative possibilities, thus destroying our peace of mind and becoming as distressed by the prospect of what might happen, as we would be if it actually did happen. Worry makes us double losers: we lose because we are relatively powerless over future eventualities, and we lose because our current well-being is compromised.

Throughout his public life and ministry, Jesus was calling people to a new way of living. Everyone who followed him would be walking a new path, living a different life, facing quite new experiences. Such a new and unpredictable lifestyle is likely to generate a degree of fear—both the instinctive, rational fear that makes us take extra care in unfamiliar situations, and the less rational fear of public failure and even ridicule.

Fear and worry are not, in principle, incompatible with the Christian call. What is incompatible however, is the paralyzing fear that immobilizes, and the chronic worry that incapacitates. The instincts of fear and worry need to be acknowledged and handled, and with a mixture of experience and trust—or faith. When Jesus says, "do not worry," on the one hand he is reassuring and encouraging, and on the other hand he is mandating something. Nor is he simply advising; he is commanding. Commands, as we have seen, not only depend on moral force or authority but must actually be possible to carry out. We *can* learn to stop worrying about certain things. Or we can at least learn to overcome the paralyzing effects of out-of-control worrying.

The response that Jesus seeks to evoke in us is not simply an issue of mind over matter: we are not called to grit our teeth, draw a deep breath, and take the plunge, step off the edge, or go over the top. The reason we can deal with worry and fear is that we know, we believe, and we trust the Jesus who calls us. We are not simply required to take initiatives but to respond to God's initiatives in our lives. But because God's call will surprise and challenge us— and sometimes make us fearful or worried—we need the conviction that the God who calls is also the God who makes things possible. "Fear not; I have overcome the world," says Jesus. *This* is the foundation of our hope.

But the command we are considering here is not simply a generic command not to worry. It is a command more tightly focused on how our lives will be lived in *witness* to the Gospel. We are not called either to completely worry-free lives or to lives that are so self-consciously controlled and contrived that fear is eliminated. That is frankly impossible. That would be to live in a world of fantasy and self-indulgence. No, we are called to live for the

Gospel, to live for others, and to live for God. Our lives as Christians have a necessarily social dimension. We have to witness to the Gospel, live for God's justice, and advocate for anyone who is victimized in any way. It is this consideration or dimension of Christianity that is illuminated by the command of Jesus, "do not worry what you are to say."

At this point in Mark's Gospel, Jesus is talking explicitly about the cost of discipleship and the price to be paid for remaining in the little company of those who follow *The Way*. He itemizes a number of things they should look out for: the seductive voices of false promises and pseudo-prophets; the rhetoric of wars to end all wars; earthquake and famine (Mk 13:5–8). And yet he says: "do not be alarmed" (Mk 13:7). He foresees that his disciples will be called before religious authorities or punished by tribunals, and that they will be led away or handed over to civil or monarchical powers (Mk 13:9–10). And still he says, "Do not worry about what you are to say" (Mk 13:11). Many translations, including the NRSV, rightly add the word *beforehand*: "Do not worry *beforehand* what you are to say."

A further point to bear in mind, though, as we ponder this saying, is that the Christians of the first century "would have been terrified at the prospect of having to defend themselves in a public trial."[1] So the point is not that there should be no fear, but that *debilitating, destructive* fear can be relieved.

We can identify two important considerations. First, Jesus is saying: live your life; live for the present; live with a degree of equanimity and peace; do not fail to live fully in the here and now. And then he is making a promise, a promise that will help his followers to do what he commands: he says "it is not you who speak, but the Holy Spirit" (Mk 13:11). This point, of course, is absolutely critical, both for Jesus and his original audience, and for those early Christians.

Luke says, "Do not panic" (21:9), which is even more forceful and evocative of people's likely response to situations of enormous stress, and rather more immediate than Jesus' words in the *King*

James translation of Matthew, a somewhat laid-back "do not be troubled" (Mt 24:6).

Luke also elaborates on Mark, having Jesus say in the *Jerusalem Bible* translation: "I will give you eloquence" (Lk 21:15).[2] The Word promises to put words in the mouths of disciples. Earlier, Jesus had promised that "the Holy Spirit will teach you…what you ought to say" (Lk 12:11–12).

So now, at last, what Jesus is saying makes some sense to would-be disciples. Indeed, it makes full sense only because of this assurance of the Holy Spirit. We Christians say that we believe in the Holy Spirit, and yet time and time again we demonstrate just how unconvincing we are—to ourselves and to others—as a Spirit-led people and a Spirit-led Church. Even when we are fired up with commitment and conviction, we so often act as if everything depended on ourselves. But Jesus is trying to make us pay attention, and to understand and act differently. He is reiterating that God's Spirit is in charge of the enterprise, and that nothing can prevail against the Spirit. But we have to listen, to believe, and to allow the Spirit to work.

We live in a world of change and paradox, of unconscionable injustice and unbounded promise. Some of us are so easily tempted by undreamed of possibilities or seduced by siren voices, while others may be paralyzed into inactivity or made cynical by the evil and injustice all around. Perhaps it was ever thus. But we are called to be disciples. Disciples must not succumb to the world, the devil, or the flesh; neither must they be cowed by fear or overcome by worry. The way forward is challenging, for it is the narrow way of Jesus. We cannot simply look for the quiet life and keep out of trouble. Jesus calls for disciples who are witnesses or martyrs: and we must respond, at the cost of comfort and even of life, but on the conviction that the Spirit will, can, and must speak in and through us.

We might notice that not only does Jesus issue commands; he very often accompanies them with words of encouragement or qualification. In the present case he says do not worry "beforehand." In

other words, live your life with a degree of serenity and trust: worrying in advance does little to help anyone, and may distract us
from important matters of the moment. But—and this is critically
important—Jesus also addresses his disciples directly, saying, "Do
not worry about what you are to say." He is not talking about worrying what they will actually say, but what they *should* say, what
they *are to say*. He is not talking about their own words or their
own verbal dexterity or appropriateness: he is alerting them to the
fact that God will be speaking through them. He is promising that
"what [they] are to say" is what God, or God's Spirit, wants to say
through them. Let them not worry: the words are of God; the words
are God's; and the words will be put in their mouths when the
time comes. How do we know this? Because Jesus himself says it
immediately afterwards: "Say *whatever is given you at that time, for
it is not you who speak, but the Holy Spirit*" (Mk 13:11, italics mine).
Given this promise, the command itself becomes not only much
easier for us to obey, but most encouraging—for those who have
faith—to receive.

In our own time, the verbally dexterous and the well-coached
"spin doctors" are in the ascendancy. Politicians are not the only
"politically correct" people, not the only ones who know how to
say the right thing at the right time; there are deceivers in the
Church as well. Behind some of their words is a culture of un-
truth, a platform (political and even ecclesiastical) built on lies.
Sometimes, when the lies are uncovered, the liars try to justify themselves by saying their words were necessary *so that people would
not worry*. More often, perhaps, they have been carefully woven as
a cover for the liar, in the hopes that his (usually his) lying will
serve to postpone his worries. The message of Jesus is quite different and very challenging: "the truth will set you free," he asserts;
and for those who really trust and try to walk in the truth, "do not
worry about what you are to say." It sounds very encouraging, but
it calls for great integrity and immense trust.

∼

PRAYER

God, our life and strength,
remind us of your promises,
remind us of your love.

Your Beloved Son Jesus
reminded us that words will be given us.
He promised that your Holy Spirit
would speak your truth through us.

When we are worried, calm our souls.
When we are afraid, strengthen our resolve.
When we are mute, give us your words.
When we babble, teach us silence.

Then, Lord God, we will be
neither tongue-tied nor talkers of nonsense,
but the mouthpiece of your truth,
the medium of your good news.

Questions

1. Am I troubled or a worrier? Dare I meditate on the *command* not to be?
2. Can I rate myself on a fear-scale of 1 to 10? If "perfect love casts out fear," what do I need to pay attention to?
3. Do I encourage others not to fear? At what personal cost?

Endnotes

1. John R. Donohue and Daniel Harrington, *The Gospel of Mark*. Collegeville, Minn.: Michael Glazier/Liturgical Press, 2002, p. 370.
2. Luke Timothy Johnson, *The Gospel of Luke*. Collegeville, Minn.: Michael Glazier/Liturgical Press, 1991, p. 322.

7

"FOLLOW ME"

Luke 5:27

I n Luke's Gospel, "follow me," is first addressed to Levi. The evangelist immediately continues, "He got up, left everything, and followed him." Thinking of this commandment ("follow me"), many of us might first recall the occasion, recorded very early in Mark's Gospel, in which Jesus calls Simon and Andrew, the fishermen brothers, with the words, "Follow me *and I will make you fish for people*" (Mk 1:17, italics mine). But we must not think that the only outcome of following Jesus is a human catch in this sense: the fishing metaphor simply identifies one possible outcome. Luke had Mark's earlier account available to him, yet seems to have deliberately chosen *not* to use it here.

In my youth I enjoyed walking the countryside of England and Scotland. By my third and fourth decade, the walking became more taxing as I trekked from village to village in West Africa. It was still enjoyable, but the burning midday heat, the vast low-lying swamps, the narrow tracks or footpaths, the steep hillsides—and the dense undergrowth and plentiful snakes—constituted an unfamiliar challenge. Added to this, I simply did not know the way from one village to the next, for there were no signposts and no roads. In such circumstances it was necessary to take "guides"— only-too-willing schoolboys who would help carry camp bed, bedding, Mass-kit, and clothes (and who knew they would be fed well and treated hospitably, at our destination). There were usually four or five of us, and it was impossible to walk side by side. I could walk ahead, but did not know where we were going, so that was futile. I could try to find my own path, but was irrationally afraid of snakes, so that was stupid. Gradually I discovered that I needed to follow the leader. By trial and error I learned that the best way to follow was effectively to walk in the footsteps of the one who went before me: he was invariably more surefooted than me, more able to identify the best way through a muddy stretch or up the side of a challenging hill. And yet I never quite overcame the desire to be more independent, more able to make my own choices. Almost always I was wrong whenever I did.

Now, living through Chicago winters, I have learned how much easier it is, and how much more sensible, to follow in the footsteps of one who has tracked through the snow before me than to step into the "deep and crisp and even," which is either deeper than the height of my shoes or frozen solid and likely to turn an ankle. On the feast of Stephen, Good King Wenceslaus once looked out for the page who followed in his footsteps. In Sierra Leone, schoolboys always looked out for me as I tried to follow in theirs. But the one whom we are called to follow as if our lives depend on it is the one who says, "Come, follow me."

There are two kinds of New Testament situations—sometimes overlapping—in which "following" is emphasized. Quite often, the evangelists simply tell us that someone (or a group or crowd) follows Jesus, apparently of their own accord, perhaps more out of curiosity than commitment. At other times, Jesus expressly bids, or commands, someone to follow him. But there is one further significant occasion where following is involved: before healing the official's daughter, "Jesus got up *and followed him, with his disciples*" (Mt 9:19, italics mine). Jesus, who calls others to follow, is sensitive and obedient enough to know when it is appropriate for him to follow. In fact, his whole life is a *response*, a following, of the will of his *abba*. Even the decisions Jesus makes should not be seen simply as initiatives on his part: repeatedly in the space of two chapters, the Jesus of John's Gospel reminds his disciples that his own will is expressly to do the will of his Father (see Jn 4:34; 5:30; 6:38). This point is worth returning to later, as we seek further insight for our own discipleship and following of Jesus.

We may begin by reminding ourselves of the occasions on which Jesus actually says, "Follow me." When someone (Matthew refers to him as a *disciple,* perhaps implying that more was expected of him) wanted to bury his father, Jesus said, "Follow me, and let the dead bury their own dead" (Mt 8:22). This seems rather cold and brusque, and it may be an embarrassment to those who want to dull the sharp edge of Jesus' words. But it certainly identifies the immediacy and emergency that Jesus associates with following him: time is short and the demands of the kingdom cannot wait. This particular form of the command "follow me" has produced lively debate over the centuries. As expectations of the imminent return of Jesus were modified, not surprisingly the sense of emergency and immediacy evaporated. But at the very least, this stark and challenging saying warrants our own meditation and does not justify our quick dismissal of its demand. Following Jesus is never like a walk in the country; it always calls for self-denial and willingness to take up our cross.[1]

After Peter's profession of faith (and a manifestation of his dangerous tendency to want Jesus to conform to his idea of a conquering hero), Jesus attempted to warn him and the others "that he must go to Jerusalem and undergo great suffering at the hands of the elders and chief priests and scribes, and be killed" (Mt 16:21). Peter simply could not accept this, and a heated argument ensued. Jesus warned Peter not to become "a stumbling block [scandal][2] to me," and reiterated the demands of discipleship: "If any want to become my followers, let them deny themselves and take up their cross and follow me" (Mt 16:24). Leaving nothing to chance, he then proceeded to speak about saving and losing one's life. This is a far cry from "fishing for people": it is explicitly about following Jesus to his death. Like Peter, many of us may not be able to accept the demands of discipleship, even though we *know* that *The Way* of Jesus led to his death, even though we have heard and spoken the conditions of discipleship many times. As we reflect on the call to "follow me," we may need to ask God for a portion of courage, to stiffen our resolve.

A third occasion is the encounter between Jesus and the rich (young) man. Having been asked directly what he (the rich man) must do to inherit eternal life, Jesus tells him to go, sell everything, give to the poor, "then come, follow me" (Mt 19:21; Mk 10:21). Here is someone who believes he is good and faithful, and indeed Jesus commends him and loves him. But since the man asked, Jesus told him: "You lack one thing." This is both an amazing endorsement (if we thought we lacked *only one thing*, we would be thrilled), and a call to radical discipleship. The man is called to go even beyond obedience to the law and to commit himself to an explicit following of Jesus. But here, "follow me" is preceded by four other commands: "go, sell, give, come." It is rather too much for this good man. However, recalling this encounter might remind us that sometimes we, too, look for clarity, for (simple) rules of observance ("what must I do?"), rather than dare to risk, to trust, and to follow. Sometimes, cutting our own path or going our own way is much easier; it is also more self-motivated or self-interested, and less faithful to the one who calls.

As far as following Jesus is concerned, the Gospel of John provides us with an interesting contrast and a splendid opportunity for reflection. The first disciples are *not* initially called by Jesus, and *not* commanded to follow him. The contours of the attraction, the invitation, and the commitment are quite different from what the Synoptic accounts give us. John's Gospel first tells us of certain disciples of John the Baptist (Andrew and Simon Peter), who more or less invite themselves to follow Jesus, although, when they ask where he is staying, he does say, "Come and see." The following day Jesus does call someone, but not one of those who came to him: John's Gospel says simply, "He found Philip and said to him, 'Follow me'" (Jn 1:43). It was Philip who then found Nathanael, countering the latter's hesitation with the same words that Jesus had used to invite Andrew and Simon: "Come and see."

This whole episode is striking because it indicates that people can be called indirectly or by others, but it also reveals the common thread: the initiative or invitation of Jesus. Here, however, there is no talk of denying self or of taking up a cross. Instead, we see a number of components that fit together to produce a picture of incipient discipleship: the enthusiasm of the would-be disciples; the encouragement of Jesus (accompanied by gratuitous statements and promises); the direct call by Jesus (in contrast to the rich man's personal initiative); the "contagious" attraction of Jesus; and the insight and affirmation of Jesus. First, Jesus changes Simon's name to Peter; then Jesus calls Philip; then Philip draws Nathanael; then Jesus validates and confirms Nathanael. Meanwhile, Andrew named Jesus "Rabbi" and "Messiah"; Philip identified Jesus as the one written about by Moses and the prophets; and Nathanael called him "Rabbi," "Son of God," and "King of Israel"! On top of all this, Jesus begins to disclose something very important ("you will see greater things"), and makes amazing promises ("you will see heaven opened and the angels of God ascending and descending upon the Son of Man"), turning these near-strangers into followers. It is all very intense, and intensely exciting, not only for those immediately involved but for those of us who dare to ponder these dynamics and apply these promises to ourselves as we try to follow Jesus.

Finally, we must reflect on the implication of that final encounter between Simon Peter and Jesus, recorded in John's Gospel. Peter has betrayed Jesus; Jesus has been crucified; Peter has repented; and Jesus has risen. The stage is set for Peter's rehabilitation, as, gently yet firmly, Jesus repeats his earlier call. But John's Gospel did not record that call. John's Jesus allowed Simon and Andrew to follow him, and then invited them to "come and see" where he was staying. He also renamed Peter, Simon, but without any explanation. Jesus did not, in John's account, explicitly say, "Follow me." But now, by the Sea of Tiberias, Jesus asks Peter three times whether he loves him (Jn 21:15–19). And three times Peter —who denied Jesus three times—now asserts his love.

This is almost unbearably poignant, for we cannot forget the earlier occasion, not long before the betrayal, when Peter had been so adamant about his fierce faithfulness. They were at Supper, Judas had just departed on his own mission, and Jesus was talking in subdued tones about his impending betrayal and departure. He had not even finished telling his disciples of the importance of their loving one another as he loved them (Jn 13:34), when Peter was suddenly struck by what he had said. "Lord, where are you going?" he asked with breathtaking naivety. And Jesus, elliptically, replied: "Where I am going, you cannot follow me now; *but you will follow afterward*" (Jn 13:36, italics mine). At this point, Peter, to his subsequent shame, swears that he will lay down his life for Jesus.

Now it is that final day by the waterside. Peter's triple affirmation has almost erased his triple denial, and Jesus is gently reminding him that his youthful independence of spirit and choice must yield to more mature behavior. Jesus warns Peter that in the future he will be less able to determine his own movements, and that he will need to adopt a different attitude. Having spent so much time with Jesus and yet still failed to understand, Peter is getting yet another, final, lesson on discipleship. Jesus says to Peter, simply, finally, and repeatedly (for he says it twice), "Follow me" (Jn 21:19, 22). This is his very last word on the subject.

Jesus calls us to come after him and to follow him. He also shows throughout his own life how obedient he himself is, and how faithfully he follows the instructions, the will, of his *Abba*. Here is example and encouragement for us, for God is ever faithful. And as we ponder our call to follow Jesus, we should not forget that extraordinary occasion when Jesus followed the official to his home, in order to heal his slave! (Lk 7:6). Here is an illustration of what true discipleship amounts to; this is how it will be judged. The one who calls us to follow him is also one who is willing to follow someone in need. To follow Jesus is to go and do likewise.

∽

PRAYER

Lord, it's very encouraging of you
to invite me to come and follow you.
I know that you are the Way to life,
and I really want to live life to the full.

But there are at least three problems:
I am frequently afraid of your demands;
I would sometimes like to go my own way;
and the cross seems unavoidable.

If there's a solution for every problem,
then I really need your reassurance;
I really need your help;
I really need your courage.

So, Lord, don't just call me.
Jesus, please don't just command.
Let your Spirit be my guide,
and let your promise be my strength.

Questions

1. What qualities would it take for me to follow someone?
2. How much would I need to know in advance?
3. Am I deliberately trying to follow Jesus?
4. What's the biggest surprise I ever received as a follower?

Endnotes

1. See the reflection on this in the chapter, "Deny Yourself."
2. See the reflection on scandal in the chapter, "Tear Your Eye Out."

8

"GIVE THEM SOMETHING TO EAT YOURSELVES"

Mark 6:37

Mark the Evangelist does not waste words, though sometimes he may seem to: he likes to plant a little seed in his readers' or hearers' minds, and later, when we have almost forgotten it, he returns to visit it and see what has happened to it. The command of Jesus that we turn to now illustrates this strategy very well.

After Jesus raised the twelve-year-old girl to life (Mk 5:21–43),[1] he left her astonished family with two commands: he "strictly ordered them that no one should know [what had happened], and he told them to give her something to eat." The first of these commands relates to the "Messianic Secret," according to which Jesus refused to appear like a modern-day celebrity, much less as a miracle-worker, but wanted to draw people by degrees, to real faith and mature discipleship. But as long as he was restoring people to life or producing other dramatic "deeds of power," it was clearly quite unrealistic to expect people to keep quiet. Whether or not they were developing authentic Messianic expectations, they were certainly not so nonchalant as to be unaffected or uninterested in the kinds of things Jesus was (reputed to be) doing. Therefore, not only would Jesus inevitably continue to attract crowds of people, including the merely curious and the frankly cynical, but his reputation would grow by the day. Far from keeping quiet, people were abuzz with excitement.

As to the second command: the girl's family would presumably be quite compliant, positively hurrying to give the girl something to eat, so excited would they be at her recovery. Dead people do not eat: Jesus would remind his closest followers of this after his own resurrection when he met them on the shore (Lk 24:42; Jn 21:12). So, this girl did not merely *appear* to be alive: she was alive, and hungry, too! But perhaps even more importantly, by telling the parents to feed their daughter, Jesus is ensuring that the family is not simply passive recipients of his deed of power. He wants the parents to participate actively in their daughter's restoration and well-being. Feeding her is a very simple and typical way for them to be involved. He could easily have done it for them, but he chose not to do so. They were her parents. They had responsibilities and indeed resources.

With these thoughts in mind, we—modern-day readers of these old, yet timeless, stories—can follow the evangelist Mark as he brings his own audience to the next stage of his narrative. Having acknowledged that Jesus was "amazed" at the lack of faith of the general populace (Mk 6:6)—an observation that contrasts so markedly with the much more positive amazement of the Gerasene community (Mk 5:20) and the family of the little girl (Mk 5:42)—Jesus then gathered his Twelve, and sent them out two by two. Upon their return he called them to withdraw a little in order to catch their breath. In such circumstances as these, he was as concerned for their well-being as he was for his own, for he knew just how demanding the apostolate could be. So, as the *Jerusalem Bible* says, they rowed or sailed to "a lonely place where they could be by themselves" (Mk 6:32). But not for long; people saw them leaving, and many anticipated where they were going, and soon Jesus and his little band were again surrounded by growing crowds.

The immediate response of Jesus shows how big was his

pastoral heart. Although he wanted to be alone, and particularly to give his disciples some respite, his compassion for the aimless and leaderless crowds led him to address their needs and, as the *Jerusalem Bible* says, "to teach them at some length" (Mk 6:24).

The disciples, however, are not quite so compassionate or pastoral: they seem to be more concerned for their own "quiet time" and for claiming Jesus for themselves. Mark (in the *Jerusalem Bible* translation) portrays them as eminently reasonable and practical: "His disciples came up to him and said, 'This is a lonely place, and it is getting very late; so *send them away,* and they can go into the farms and villages round about, to buy themselves something to eat'" (Mk 6:36). But this reasonable-sounding statement masks a couple of rather significant issues. It also demonstrates the gap between the would-be disciples and true disciples according to Jesus' standards.

In the first place, when "it is getting very late" in Mediterranean countries, it will very soon be dark: there is little or no twilight, and of course no artificial lighting. Consequently, people would not want to be far from home or from a place to sleep. Moreover, "villages" are few and far between. So it seems that the disciples are in fact *not* being realistic, or helpful. Furthermore, we discover quite soon that it was not true that it is late (as the NRSV states), much less "very late" (according to the *Jerusalem Bible*). For after his encounter with this crowd, Jesus will send the disciples on ahead in the boat, say good-bye to the crowds, and go off to the hills to pray—and only after all that, Mark tells us, is it evening time! (Mk 6:47).

The second issue is even more significant as far as the command of Jesus is concerned. It is that the disciples fail, or refuse, to take any responsibility for the crowds. They expect Jesus to do everything. Given their recent commissioning (Mk 6:7–13), this represents a serious dereliction of duty. Their phrase, "send them away," bespeaks a complete lack of true concern and no sense of responsibility. This is not the first time, nor will it be the last, that the closest disciples of Jesus try to get rid of people or avoid taking responsibility (as with the Caananite woman [Mt 15:23]; or Bartimaeus [Mk 10:48]).

Against this background and these circumstances, the force of Jesus' words can now be fully felt: give them something to eat yourselves, he says (Mk 6:37). Jesus is neither a fool nor a cynic: he knows quite well that the disciples do not have a commissariat or food repository nearby, and he is surely not just carping at their lack of social responsibility. And yet he speaks these words, which constitute a command. As we ponder the command and its implications and applications, we will learn some profound truths about discipleship and about Jesus.

Disciples of Jesus are called to come to him, to learn from him, to follow him, and to continue his works (Jn 14:12). Disciples are not to sit around, not to remain passive recipients, and not to wait for Jesus to do everything that needs to be done. The starkness and directness of these words, therefore, cannot fail to strike us: Give them something to eat yourselves. What do these words imply?

If commands are to be carried out, they must not entail conditions that are impossible to fulfill. Jesus is issuing a command here; therefore it must at least be possible for the disciples to give them something to eat. They are not destitute, not without imagination, and not without resources, however meager these may seem. What the disciples are required to do, therefore, is to be responsible, generous, creative, and trusting. If they have a sense of responsibility they will realize that they must do something even though they cannot do everything. If they are generous (and if they have learned anything at all from Jesus, and if they have any sense of integrity or honor), they will know that they simply cannot think of themselves and be egotistical in these circumstances. If they are creative they will not be imprisoned by what is, but will ask themselves—and perhaps others—"what if?" ("What if we all share?") If they have developed any degree of trust they will act as if they believe Jesus will not abandon them now. But perhaps the most important insight to be derived from this command is that it causes people—disciples, ourselves—to realize that they do indeed possess *some* resources, *some* capacity, *some* possibilities for action, *and that they are required to believe that this is so, and to act on it.*

Thirty years ago when I was working in Sierra Leone, West Africa, I found myself in an isolated and relatively poor part of the country. The "parish" was very extensive and comprised more than two hundred villages. Access was by foot. After several months of trekking, I had established a "circuit" of about thirty villages that could be visited on a regular basis, by myself or by the priest with whom I worked. But the upkeep of the missionaries was a major challenge for both of us.

The people had very little to eat, but they did have something, grown by their own hands in exacting circumstances. The missionaries had no homegrown food but were available to trek from village to village and preach the good news, and were seen to do so, week after week. Soon, a bargain was struck: instead of trying to rely on the classical method of exacting "monthly dues" from church members, we asked them to contribute in kind. At first the people were reluctant. But gradually they became more forthcoming. In the low season, they had little and we received less: perhaps the odd (*very* odd, on most occasions, because so scrawny) chicken. But when the harvest came in—rice, peanuts, yams, cassava—not only would the church members provide a small pan of rice, but they would compete with one another in their giving. So much did we receive that we were able to collect small amounts of rice from thirty villages, live on it through the year, and sell the excess to fund the mission. We had, explicitly, attempted to take the local people seriously and to call these disciples to account, in a realistic fashion. They in turn were not only supportive of us, but were highly pleased with themselves. This is no bad thing: the biblical virtue of almsgiving (and this is true in Zoroastrianism, Islam, and other traditions) was always understood to benefit the donor, as much as, if not more than, the recipient!

The disciples' perennial problem is that they simply do not believe that Jesus believes in them, that he takes them seriously, and that he wants them to realize their God-given potential. The problem many modern-day disciples have is exactly the same: we do not believe that God takes us seriously and that God wants us, *needs us,* to take ourselves seriously too. We are not powerless, not impotent. We *can* do something; we *must* do something; we are *commanded* to do something. The command does not focus on what we can do for ourselves, but on what we *must* do for others, for one another. This is the way the followers of Jesus are called to act. This is what changes life. This is what changes the world. Some of us fail to believe in ourselves, some fail to take God and Jesus seriously, and some are perhaps persuaded that we are insignificant. But no one is insignificant: this is at the heart of Jesus' teaching; and here is a commandment that, if implemented, could change lives, would certainly change the church, and might even change the world.

Too many of us are either full of good intentions (procrastinators or not in touch with reality) or too easily persuaded that there is nothing we can do. Just because we cannot do everything is no excuse for not doing something. And there is *always* something we can do if we put our mind, our imagination, and our heart into it.

We pray, we worship, and we say we believe. Yet so little seems to change in our lives and, consequently, so little changes in a world deprived of justice and the basic stuff of survival. Next time we read, or hear, or think about the parents of the twelve-year-old girl raised by Jesus or the disciples surrounded by a huge crowd of hungry people, perhaps we will remember the command: it comes from Jesus and it applies to a world that is hungry for bread and for justice, for drink and for mercy, for dignity and for hope: "Give them something to eat yourselves." Isn't today a good time to take this commandment more seriously?

~

Prayer

Bounteous, bountiful God,
all we have comes from you.
You feed our hunger and assuage our thirst,
but you leave us still more hungry and thirsty
for your justice.

What can we do in return?
How can we show our gratitude?
How shall we speak when we are dumb?
What can we give when our hands are empty?

To his first disciples Jesus said,
give them something to eat yourselves,
and they found invisible resources
and discovered the power of sharing.

To us, today, his words are no less clear:
from our poverty we must give;
from our lack we must share.
God will give the increase because God can.
We will receive because we can learn graciousness.
Others will benefit because they are in need.

But all, together, are required:
No one can stand apart or independent.
Mutual indebtedness binds our communities,
making meaning from our lives.

Questions

1. God takes me very seriously. God chooses to need me. Do I believe this?
2. Can I identify two or three gifts, resources, or talents that I can share with others?
3. It is simply not true that I can do nothing: there is always *something* I can do. What will I do today? Or what will I fail to do?

Endnotes

1. See Chapter Four, "Do Not Fear, Only Believe."

9

"Go Home to Your People and Tell Them"

Mark 5:19

S ome people, deeply committed to Jesus, seem not really to have considered the missionary component of discipleship. They imagine there are two very different kinds of Christians: missionaries and others. Missionaries, they think, leave home and travel great distances to preach the Good News and build up the Church. The rest of Christians—the others—are "the faithful." They stay home, living quiet and inconsequential lives.

Yes, there is exaggeration here! But Vatican II reminded us of the essential missionary nature of baptism: that it is by virtue of baptism that we are co-missioned, and that if we claim to be *confirmed* in that baptism (which is the meaning of the sacrament of confirmation), then we have chosen to activate that missionary component. Yet, even forty years after the Council, there are still many, many people who declaim modestly, "O, I'm not a missionary."

There are at least three things wrong with this assertion. First, it indicates a poor understanding of "missionary"; second, it shows an impoverished comprehension of baptism; and third, it betrays a very limited grasp of discipleship itself. Let's look at the last of these: later we will consider the others. Discipleship entails, first, the call by Jesus, then the commissioning ("co-missioning") by Jesus, and then the following of Jesus. Those who aspire to being true and radical disciples will undertake a certain amount of "leaving," as well as an acceptance of hardship as part of the cost of discipleship. But "leaving" and "hardship" cannot be exactly measured. What we can do is identify a certain minimum requirement, which brings us to the commandment under review here. Like the others that we are considering, this one too has a universal applicability. It reflects the very missionary dimension of discipleship ("Go"...tell [the good news]"). But the particular circumstances of its utterance are also worth some serious reflection.[1]

Jesus was passing through the land of the Gerasenes when a crazed man, evidently living in a graveyard, saw him from a distance, ran toward him, threw himself at his feet, and shouted in a very loud voice (Mk 5:6–7). There are other examples of dramatic encounters between Jesus and assorted people but surely none as striking as this, for the apparently demented man addressed his remarks very explicitly and directly, to "Jesus, Son of the most High God." Here is a pariah, a social outcast, someone not merely on the edges of society but as good as dead (he lives among the tombs, among the dead, and thus is himself "socially dead"); yet he identifies Jesus unambiguously and in words that illustrate his incipient *faith*. Here is a basis on which Jesus can build, a foundation on which he will reconstruct this nameless man's life. And when that has been done, Jesus will commission, as the *Jerusalem Bible* puts it, yet one more disciple, with the words: "Go home to your people, and tell them all that the Lord in his mercy has done for you." These are surely words for us to live by, too.

Elie Wiesel, survivor of Auschwitz and a man who effectively ceased to believe in God after the Holocaust, returned to the faith of his fathers and mothers in later life. In one of his books, he reflects on the notion of conversion, and on its meaning in his own life.[2] The Hebrew word is *teshuvah*, the root of which is *shub*, meaning literally "to return home." But God is the implied agent, or initiator: it is God who turns a person homeward.

Many Christians are considerably more familiar with the Greek word *metanoia* as the basis of our understanding of conversion. *Metanoia* has something to do with changing one's mind (from the root *nous/noia,* which means "the mind"), and the active agent seems to be the self (*I* change *my* mind). Many of us may have located the idea of conversion in our own head. But to return home requires in the first instance that we move our feet! It also presupposes that we *remember* where home actually is, that we have previous knowledge and experience on which to draw, and that we now have some reason that is more persuasive than the reason we left in the first place! In the story of the Prodigal Son (Lk 15:11–32), the moment of truth arrives precisely when the young man decides to return home (Lk 15:20). This is the moment of conversion, and it is met and acknowledged by the father's tender embrace, hearty welcome, forgiveness, and the rehabilitation of his son (Lk 15:20–24). Conversion, then, is not measured simply by returning home, but both by the reason or impulse behind it, and by its consequences.

With these thoughts in mind, we can return to the present story, and to the final instructions of Jesus to the man he has restored to sanity: "Go [back] home to your people, and tell them all that the Lord in his mercy has done for you." This is not only a call to conversion but affirmation and empowerment too. But there will be a further twist.

The dramatic encounter between Jesus and the anonymous disturbed man ("Legion" is how he identifies himself, indicating what we might call a split personality or a man with a multiple identity) takes place neither in the tombs nor in the township, but out of sight of the local villagers. By the time the man is restored to health, it is very much at the expense of an enormous herd of some two thousand pigs.[3] Local swineherds are the only witnesses, perhaps not to the encounter between Jesus and "Legion," but certainly to the terrifying spectacle of the panicked pigs rushing headlong for the cliff. Not surprisingly, those pigkeepers were in a very emotional state when they ran back to the town to spread the bad news.

According to the storyteller, the curious townspeople were primarily impressed by the dramatic change in the madman's demeanor. No longer wild and crazed, he was sitting quite still, in his full senses, and was also—and inexplicably—"clothed." This was already too much for them, "and they were afraid." Afraid of what, exactly? René Girard[4] suggests that the root of their fear was their realization that they could no longer categorize—and thus control—the crazy man. Nor could they any longer sustain their codependency or facilitation of him and his wild, lawless, and self-destructive condition. He was now *out* of the graveyard and the tombs, *in* his right mind, and *in* clothes appropriate for a "civilized" person. He was also seated and still. All this represented a complete reversal from his previous state. Previously he could be kept at arm's length, avoided, and disregarded with impunity; now, healed, he was a living rebuke to all who had callously left him to die in the graveyards. So they were afraid; and with good reason.

It is only at this point that the swineherds report the fate of the pigs. No wonder the community moves beyond simple fear: they now implore Jesus "to leave their neighborhood" (Mk 5:17). This man Jesus is not only changing the social organization, he is undermining the economic structures as well, not to mention wielding great and fearsome power, power such as they have never encountered.

We recall that wherever he goes, Jesus is looking for faith or bringing people to faith, though he never uses coercive power. So, at the bidding of the frightened and resistant community, Jesus does indeed prepare to leave. But as he was getting into the boat, the healed man takes on a much more active role than before. His attitude is in stark counterpoint to that of everyone else. *They* beg Jesus to leave; *he* begs to be allowed to stay with Jesus. But, curiously, while Jesus accedes to the desires of the townspeople, he refuses the request of the man he has just cured.

Now, as all the pieces of this drama come together in the climactic moment, we who read the story can identify them and see how they fit in the context of the puzzle that is our own lives. Are we perhaps "living in the graveyard," neither fully alive nor truly dead—but perhaps a little closer to death than to life? Are we able to identify Jesus as "Son of the Most High God"—or do we see him only as a distant figure, if not an irritation or a reproach? Are we afraid: afraid that our comfortable and predictable lives might be challenged and changed if we were to allow Jesus to come too close to where we live? Do we want to be left in peace, to be left to our own devices, and in this way to keep Jesus out of the neighborhood like the villagers in this story? Or do we, perhaps, like the protagonist here, find ourselves restored, in our right mind, and really wanting to follow Jesus? Are we ready to respond to the impulse of God and retrace our steps, to return home, and, if necessary, to face the music?

What Jesus does next is very interesting and illustrative. He turns to the expectant would-be disciple and says: "Go home to your people," and "tell them how much the Lord in his mercy has done for you." What a command! What a commission! "Go," is one of the most significant words in Jesus' vocabulary, and it is concentrated, monosyllabic, empowering. It is a *performative* word: one that actually sends a person forth, actually commissions.

In this particular case, however, he does not simply command the man to go, but specifically *to go home,* and to go to his own people. Here is the impulse, the agency, the encouragement, and the empowerment. To go home, to return home, evokes that image of conversion. Jesus is not setting the act of going home in opposition to the act of following him; they are essentially the same thing, provided the outcome is commitment to seeking the reign of God. Some people explicitly follow Jesus on *The Way,* seeking to accompany him and be led by him (the emphasis may be more on the word "come" than on the word "go," although there is indeed movement *on to and along The Way of Jesus*). Others are commissioned to go, but insofar as they go in accordance with the command of Jesus, they are indeed going *his Way* rather than their own. In this particular case, the man is commissioned to return home, not for a quiet life but to evangelize his own people: this, too, is a critical component of *The Way* of Jesus.

However much we might want to identify with this newly commissioned man, we will recall that his own people were afraid, both of him and of Jesus (Mk 5:15, 17). But Jesus had already left, which means that the wounded man, now healed, had to take his courage in both hands and become a *healed healer*. We are left to ponder the amazing change that has taken place, not only in the man sent to his people but to the people to whom he is sent—for the story concludes with the observation that "everyone was amazed," implying that they were affected by the "amazing grace" that touched many lives. The text (NRSV) says the man "went away and began to proclaim in the Decapolis how much Jesus had done for him" (Mk 5:20). So, not only did he go to his own people and presumably find them sympathetic; he traveled through *ten cities*: and "everyone was amazed." Who would have imagined that such a crazy person could be rehabilitated, called, and commissioned! Such is the power of grace, when it encounters willing people. There is hope for us yet.

It is important for us to ponder the *missionary* nature of this call and command. The man can stand for *Everyman* (including every woman). Every one of us, Christian disciples, is called to "go and tell" our family, friends, neighbors, and not-so-neighbors the good news that is the inspiration of our own lives. We may not all go overseas, or go explicitly to baptize and makes disciples (the "Great Commission" of Matthew 28 was *not* addressed to everyone but explicitly to the Eleven): but we *are* called by baptism and strengthened, commissioned, and *confirmed* by confirmation, to be disciples. That means we must follow Jesus and *do what Jesus did*, each in our own milieu, each according to our own capacity and generosity of spirit. We must, in other words, go to the people and, sometimes in words but always in deed, proclaim the good news of the kingdom, which is proclaimed by witness and dialogue and liberation, as much, if not more, than by proclamation. Not everyone is sent to the nations: but everyone is certainly sent!

∼

Prayer

God of restoration, God of healing,
remind us of unfinished business.
You made us and we belong to you,
but sometimes we break down, wear out, give up.

If we should cease to believe in ourselves,
you will still remain faithful, for you are God.
If we should cease to believe in you,
you will not cease to believe in us, for you are God.

God, ever faithful and true,
help us to believe in ourselves by believing you.
Then we will have something to tell them;
then we will become good news.

Questions

1. Baptism has a missionary dimension. What does this mean to me? Am I willing to embrace the missionary dimension of baptism?
2. Confirmation should make believers more *firm*. What needs firming up in me?
3. Do I have the courage of my convictions?

Endnotes

1. For a more extended reflection on this incident, see my *Encountering Jesus: How People Come to Faith and Discover Discipleship.* Liguori/Triumph, 2002.
2. Elie Wiesel, *Five Biblical Portraits.* 1981
3. Here is another case of hyperbole. The details in this story are significant, but cannot detain us here.
4. René Girard, "The Demons of Gerasa." In *The Scapegoat.* Baltimore, Md.: Johns Hopkins University Press, 1986, 165–84.

10

"KEEP MY COMMANDMENTS"

John 14:15

The book in your hands is only a sketchbook, filled with inadequately drawn delineations of some of the commandments of Jesus. Even a true work of art could never exhaust, or even do rough justice to, such a subject matter as this. But at the heart of the enterprise (of our entire lives, not simply of this book) is the commandment that we must consider now.

"Keep my commandments" is formulated neither as an invitation nor as a statement, but as an imperative, an order. Now, as we have observed, Jesus does not simply demand the impossible (and when he appears to do so he always provides the necessary means: he makes it possible); and the various chapters of this book consider some possibilities for undertaking various commandments. They attempt to stimulate our reflection and response, to encourage us to look again at what may indeed seem impossible, and to bring us into engagement with what Jesus asks. We cannot simply turn away or give up: that is not permissible for disciples.

Jesus issues so many commandments that we could easily be overwhelmed (and we are only considering a sample of them in these pages). But he seems to do one more thing: actually to formulate a specific command that commands us to keep the commandments! Like all the others, the context of this commandment gives it meaning. The immediate context is the Last Supper and the phrase "If you love me"; we need to explore these words and their actual meaning in order to understand their full force.

First, it is crucial that we hold the two phrases together: "if you love me" and "keep my commandments." Jesus is speaking of an *enabling* love: by virtue of this love we keep the commandments. So we must ask ourselves whether our own love of Jesus actually has the capacity to motivate and enable us in this way. Or do we try to keep the commandments in the hopes of coming to love, of proving our love, or perhaps (only) of finding favor with him? Some people obey, not out of love but out of fear. Their obedience never does produce love. Others keep the commandments (to some degree), yet never experience or even imagine a loving relationship with the one who commands. Some people indeed, pass through life without ever imagining that a loving relationship *can* develop with the one who commands.

Second, we ask: what is the force of this pair of phrases, "If you love me keep my commandments"? Our familiar translation, it transpires, may be a betrayal: this may not be a *commandment* at all. Many contemporary translations render the words as, "if you love me, *you will keep* my commandments,"[1] which clarifies what Jesus is getting at. Moloney tells us that this cluster of terms ("commandments," "word," and "words") "all ask for faith in the revelation of God in and through the word of Jesus."[2]

Jesus is calling for faith, and trust: he is calling for love.

Far from making a stark demand that we keep his commandments, Jesus is carefully telling us that our obedience will be *the outcome or fruit* of our love. He is also encouraging and planting the very seeds of that love. Immediately before and after the "command," he says: "If in my name you ask me for anything, I will do it" and "I will ask the Father, and he will give you another Advocate." That's his promise and guarantee!

How often have we been motivated by fear rather than love;

how often have we given up trying; how often have we refused the challenge (to turn the other cheek, forgive multiple times, go the extra mile, and so on)? Perhaps we have not yet begun to understand Jesus, or his demands, or his promises. But if love is the motive force of his own life (which it is), and if our keeping his commands is motivated by our love of him (which it should be), then it is surely time we noticed the kingdom, or realm, breaking through all around: it is *still* not too late for us to become disciples. Everything depends on whether we believe in Jesus' love and in our capacity to reciprocate that love. Let's look more closely at this.

"God is love," says the First Letter of John, which is simply an elaboration of its theme of love. Here are a few well-known phrases to ponder: "Whoever does not love does not know God, for God is love" (4:8); "Now by this we may be sure that we know [God], if we obey [Christ's] commandments" (2:3); "All who obey [Jesus'] commandments abide in him and he abides in them" (3:24). This short epistle is a beautiful hymn to love, and its language is rich and relational: rich, as the author heaps one phrase upon other; relational in that he speaks of the love within the Trinity as well as the love between Jesus and his followers. If we are to be emboldened to respond more generously to God's love and to commit ourselves to carrying out the commandments of Jesus, perhaps we can consider some of love's characteristics. L–O–V–E: Loyalty, Openness, Virtue, Exchange. Let us examine each of these aspects of love in the following paragraphs.

The letter "L" is for loyalty, constitutive of authentic love. In the marriage service, the couple promise to love each other ("to have and to hold") "for better, for worse, for richer, for poorer, in sickness and in health, till death do us part." They undertake to sign a blank check or a contract with a great deal of small print, not because they are irrational (though they are in love!), but because of their commitment of loyalty. Each promises to be faithful, *come what may.* And the promise of each becomes the strength of the other: knowing that a loved one promises to be dependable, dedicated, and dutiful is itself a source of encouragement and strength. Experiencing someone else's encouragement and belief can be a real *inspiration,* an actual enhancement of our own performance and even of our capacity. Jesus experiences the loyalty of his *abba*; in turn, he manifests loyalty by his commitment and obedience to his *abba's* will; and (God's) loyalty is what Jesus promises his disciples. In that final discourse on the night before he died, Jesus articulates, in multiple ways, the dimensions of his loyalty as he promises to give them anything they ask (Jn 14:14), to ensure that his Father will send "another Advocate" (Jn 14:16), and never to leave them orphans (Jn 14:18). *There's* loyalty; *there's* love!

The letter "O" is for openness, transparency, and utter lack of duplicity or hypocrisy: these qualities that Jesus expects of his followers, he palpably embodies in himself. He sometimes seems exasperated that after being with them so long, and despite all his efforts to show and tell them who he is and what he is committed to, *still* they do not understand (Jn 14:8–11). Jesus will not countenance duplicity or lack of transparency in those who follow him: their competition for high honor elicits his severe criticism, and he warns them about hypocrisy and scandal in the most direct of terms. Integrity and simplicity must be hallmarks of disciples, as they are of Jesus himself. Such openness is one more of love's many faces.

The letter "V" is for virtue. Aristotle said that there is little point in *talking about* virtue: virtue must be visible, embodied, practiced. We know what justice or truth or reconciliation means, insofar as we know people who practice these virtues. In Jesus we see virtue expressed as *dikaiosunē,* "righteousness." First and foremost, this word is used in reference to *God's righteousness,* to a God's-eye view of the world. Jesus cautions the disciples: "Unless your righteousness exceeds that of the scribes and Pharisees, you will never enter the kingdom of heaven (Mt 5:20). He is calling them to practice *God's* righteousness, not simply human justice or judgment or self-justification. Clearly he is asking the impossible— unless we love, and are enabled by Jesus himself. Aristotle's insight that virtue requires practice is echoed in more recent thinkers, who remind us that practice indeed makes virtue, just as it can make vice: Viktor Frankl observed that "to love you must choose." We who aspire to love Jesus must choose his way, his justice, day by day. Only then will we become virtuous.

The letter "E" is for exchange, or mutuality. Love is not true love unless it seeks to evoke an echo in the other. Even God wants us to respond, though—quite reasonably, perhaps—we feel we can add nothing to God. There is a wonderful passage in Augustine's *Confessions*. Speaking of and to God, he says:

> Never in need, Thou dost rejoice in gain; never covetous, Thou dost demand payment with interest. More than Thou askest is given Thee, so that Thou mayest be in debt, but who has anything which is not Thine? Thou payest debts while owing no one; remittest debts while losing nothing."[3]

Here is a splendid expression of paradox, invitation, trust— and exchange! God chooses, God wants, and God undertakes to be committed to a relationship of mutual exchange with us. Jesus simply brings the message down to earth and shows how it is to be done.

The quality of love, therefore, is expressed not through sweet words, but through steadfast, dedicated, faithful action; and none of us can yet claim that our love is adequate. But Jesus' words about keeping his commandments are predicated on the phrase (and the reality it points to): "if you love me." He tells us that we will, in fact, keep his commandments *if we love him*. This is not simply Jesus' command, but his gentle reminder of what underpins our obser- vance: love.

So often Jesus needs to remind his disciples not to be afraid, for so often fear is their—as indeed it is our own—motive force. Some- times it paralyzes; but it can also stimulate us to react, and even obey, but out of very inferior motives. As the First Letter of John reminds us, "perfect love casts out fear"; and when Jesus identifies love as the generative force of our faithful observance of his commandments, he is evidently calling us beyond fear and into a realm of intimacy and freedom. Unfortunately, this is a dimension of Christianity that does not obviously characterize many Christians. *We are called, and expected, to have a loving relationship with Jesus!*

If we keep his commandments, Jesus suggests, it is *because* we love him, and not because we fear him or the wrath of God. On the other hand, if we honestly *try* to keep the commandments, then Jesus promises his abiding and enabling presence in our lives, for such effort is one of love's baby steps. Insofar as we strive loyally and lovingly, the love that develops between ourselves and Jesus will drive fear from our lives. But insofar as our lives are still governed by fear, we still do not love Jesus.

There could be many reasons for our not loving Jesus. But one does seem to dominate the lives of serious Christians: *we don't feel worthy*, *we don't really believe* that God in Jesus loves us, *we cannot imagine* a true relationship with Jesus because it seems presumptuous, and so *we fail to try* to love, and as a consequence we fail to keep his commandments as we should. It's not bad will but bad theology that paralyzes many of us. That is one reason the author of John's Gospel is so fond of the topic of love, not only providing that long discourse after the Last Supper, but much earlier in the public ministry, when he describes Jesus telling Nicodemus that, "God so loved the world that he gave his only Son, so that everyone who believes in him may not perish but may have eternal life" (Jn 3:16). We often see this on placards at football games. We may need to ponder this commandment yet again, and absorb it more fully.

However, since such words and sentiments did not penetrate the minds and hearts of Jesus' own nearest and dearest, maybe we ourselves should not be dismayed, so much as heartened: we *are called* to love; we *are capable* of loving; and *if we love*, then we will keep the commandments. Peter, so brash and so bold, aggressively asserted his faithful love: "Though all become deserters because of you, I will never desert you"; to which Jesus soberly responded:

"Truly I tell you, this very night, before the cock crows, you will deny me three times" (Mt 26:33–34). The irony cannot have been lost on Peter when Jesus later asked him: "Do you love me more than these?" and Peter replied, "Yes, Lord; you know that I love you" (Jn 21:15). But for each of the three times that Peter had denied Jesus, he must now affirm his love. Only now is he ready and able to keep the commandments he so signally broke.

As Frankl said, "to love you must choose." Like Peter, we must choose, not only, as in his case, three times, and not even thirty three times, but thirty times thirty times: constantly and consistently. Then perhaps, fear will be cast out and our love will be in place: not perfectly, but progressively. But only then will we be able to keep the commandments of life. It's surely worth practicing, worth choosing.

~

PRAYER

"If you love me," you say.
"Of course I love you," I say.
But so did Peter….

Your is an enabling love, Lord.
You actually enable me to love you.
You actually make it, if not exactly easy,
then at least possible.

No; that's not quite right either.
You actually ask the impossible;
but you also make it possible.
There's so much paradox in it all.

One thing is becoming clear:
"Keep my commandments"
is not just an order, but a kind of promise too.
It's an enabling command. I need to think it over.

Questions

1. "If you love me, keep my commandments." An order?
2. "If you love me, you will keep my commandments." A challenge?
3. If "perfect love casts out fear," what do I need to pray for?

Endnotes

1. The future tense of the Greek word (tērēsete: observe, hold, keep) makes best sense, say commentators such as Francis Moloney (*The Gospel of John,* Michael Glazier/Liturgical Press, 1998, 405), other codices notwithstanding. The word *commandments* here (*entolas)* is the word used in reference to the Ten Commandments, but Saint Paul also uses it to mean (positive or negative) *precepts* or teachings.
2. Moloney, *loc. cit.*
3. Augustine, *Confessions,* Book 1, Chapter 4.

II

"KNOCK, AND THE DOOR WILL BE OPENED"

Matthew 7:7

This is the third component of the triple command of Jesus ("ask, seek, knock"). Reflecting on the first command, we were reminded that a person who asks is someone *who acknowledges* a degree of ignorance (which is not the same thing as stupidity). As regards the second, we know that a person who seeks actually has something particular in mind, something more that a vague notion or an aimless disposition. Such a person is at least aware of lacking something—of something not yet possessed or secured—and is motivated to obtain it. Common to both kinds of people, then, is the recognition of deficiency, need, and desire, if not immediate focus.

The final part of the command (that we should knock) is similarly addressed to people who recognize their lack of completeness or self-sufficiency. This is an important consideration for those who ponder Jesus' commandments: it is not necessary for us to have all the answers. Indeed, we are not *expected* to have all the answers; but we should be striving for focus, we ought to be looking for the right questions, and we are expected to be working on the answers. The simple fact is that we are not self-sufficient, that we don't have everything we need, and, as this command will remind us, that we have not yet "arrived."

There are perhaps three kinds of people who knock. Probably the most common would be outsiders or relative strangers, but others might be people who have locked themselves out of their own home! We usually have a key to our own residence, and therefore have no need to knock; but even key-holders can forget the key or inadvertently lock themselves out. Generally speaking, those who knock are, at least temporarily, less than self-sufficient and may be somewhat embarrassed. If we should actually be willing to knock, we are acknowledging that, for whatever reason, we are not actually "in" or "at home"; we are an outsider, a guest, a beggar; or, perhaps even, we are a returning prodigal.

There is also a third possibility, and Jesus is certainly aware of it. This is the householder or master who returns, who has no need of a key, and who knocks in the sure expectation that there will be somebody—at least a servant—waiting to open the door.

These simple thoughts may help remind us of some rather obvious but overlooked truths, and orient us to the challenge Jesus offers us here.

Whoever knocks evidently hopes—or presumes, or knows—that there is someone inside, someone beyond the door who is also willing to open it, to help, to be hospitable. Whoever knocks (even the master of the household) is looking to establish or maintain a relationship, a degree of sociability or mutuality, rather than simply to assert self-sufficiency or complete independent-spiritedness.

But as we ponder the command to knock, and some of its implications, we might consider a previous observation, one that occurred in the context of Jesus' commandment that we should ask. Jesus promised that those who asked would *be given*. To be able to receive we must first be willing to ask. But some people *refuse* to ask, or seem quite incapable of asking: they simply cannot acknowledge their incompleteness or need. We also saw that in order to find, a person must not only be willing to seek but must have some

sense of direction. But some people *refuse* to seek: they do not want
to acknowledge either that they have lost something or that they
are actually lost themselves. To ask and to seek, therefore, require a
willingness to be part of society, part of a community, and not
simply to live as an isolated individualist. So, now, when we come
to reflect on those who knock, we can be ready for the same kind
of insight: to be able (willing) to knock, we must *admit* our outsider status or our forgetfulness. Some people, however, simply
refuse to do so; they would stand outside all night rather than show
their neediness. We may need to look a little more closely at our
own dispositions.

No doubt we would claim that we would never be so obstinate
as this. But what about the times in our lives when we have been
afraid to "knock" (metaphorically, if not literally), for fear of disturbing someone, or for fear of being criticized, or even out of a
sense of our own unworthiness? Obstinacy is not the only issue
here. How many of us would never think of "knocking" when "Father" was in the parish house having a rest, or when a "Do Not
Disturb" sign barred our way, or when we are intimidated by someone? How many of us have failed to act because we were afraid of
the possible consequences, although we tried to rationalize our
cowardice by claiming that we did not want to inconvenience someone else? For those of us with such experience, there is a dimension of this commandment of Jesus that should be particularly
encouraging: this command also implies that we have *permission*
to knock. It may give us the courage of our wavering convictions.

We may need to take this command very seriously, as a coun-
terbalance to our tendency to be obstinate. Or perhaps we need a
little encouragement because we are rather too diffident, too fearful, too concerned *not* to make a nuisance of ourselves. In that
case, we can hear the words, "knock, and the door will be opened
to you," in a new way. There always seems to be a degree of invitation and encouragement in the commandments of Jesus. We are
invited to take him very seriously. Far from making us embarrassed
about knocking, he indicates that he *expects* us to knock. And if

that is what he expects of us, then he will surely find a way to let us in. The times we live in demand determination and persistence, *more* knocking on *more* doors, including the doors of episcopal residences and curial offices, in God's name.

We have probably seen Holman Hunt's classic Victorian painting, *"I Stand at the Door and Knock."* We may not, however, have noticed exactly what it portrays. That would be a pity. Unfortunately the artist depicts Jesus in that rather off-putting, wistful style, characteristic of the Pre-Raphaelite Brotherhood of painters, of which he was a founding member. Still, there is depth and quality in the painting. Jesus, gentle, immaculate, crowned and robed, with a lantern in his hand, stands before a large oaken door. Not by chance, there is neither knob nor handle on the door, and not even a keyhole. Evidently, the only way for Jesus to enter—other than by force, which is clearly inappropriate—is if someone already inside is willing to open it for him. Jesus needs assistance, collaboration, community, and he himself is palpably willing to seek, to ask, and to knock, in order to find it. Hunt is surely reminding us that if Jesus is willing, then we are certainly not demeaned if we do likewise.

It is worth pondering this image of Jesus. The phrase, "I am standing at the door, knocking" (NRSV) comes from a passage in the Book of Revelation (3:20) in which Christ is speaking to various communities. He stands at the door; we stand in the position of the householder. It is one thing for us to be consoled by his promise to open the door to us; but we also have a responsibility to open the door to *him.*

The willingness to open to others who knock, which is the correlative of our own obligation to knock on other's doors, is a theme that we can identify elsewhere in Matthew's Gospel, and in two dramatic images in particular. In one, having spoken about signs that will accompany his return, Jesus says (of the Son of Man): "When you see all these things, you know that he is near, *at the very gates"* (Mt 24:33, italics mine). Authentic disciples must be sure to open those gates, to invite him in, and to show appropriate hospitality.

The other image is from the account of the Last Judgment (Mt 25:35–36), when Jesus promises to reward those who were appropriately responsive to the hungry and the thirsty, the naked and the sick, the stranger and the prisoner: precisely the kinds of people who may stand at our own door and knock. They are often invisible, of course, and they do not always knock on the actual doors of our residences; but unless the doors of our hearts resonate with their knocking, and unless we open our lives to them, we risk being excluded from the portals of paradise. It is surely good to remember that Jesus invites us to ask, to seek, or to knock, and that the invitation is backed up by the promises to respond. But we cannot afford to forget that we have the obligation of extending the favor to others.

There are few other biblical references to doors, and to knocking and opening, but they may extend our meditation on the particular command considered here. There is only one in the Old Testament, but it is provocative and evocative. In the Song of Solomon (Song of Songs), one of the lovers (the young woman) cries out, "Listen! my beloved is knocking." She has just retired for the night, but as he knocks, he whispers, "Open to me, my sister, my love, my dove, my perfect one." How could she resist? But evidently she is a little slow, for when she does open the door he has gone (Song 5:2–6). Too late! Roland Murphy writes: "The lover is no longer there, and the search begins again. There is no quick discovery [this time], and an appeal is made to the daughters to join in the search."[1] The point for us perhaps is this: in our own lives we must be attentive to the God who knocks, but equally willing *to continue* to respond, to seek, and to ask.

In the New Testament, Jesus himself elaborates on the simple injunction to knock. Talking about being in a state of readiness, he commands his disciples to "be like those who are waiting for their master to return from the wedding banquet, so that they may open the door for him as soon as he comes and knocks" (Lk 12:36). Again, disciples must not be like the foolish bridesmaids who, through their own fault, found the door closed to them (Mt 25:10–

11). Jesus is warning his followers that they must be careful not to waste their opportunities and then at the last moment to come knocking, expecting an unqualified welcome. "Strive to enter through the narrow door; for many, I tell you, will try to enter and will not be able," he says. "When once the owner of the house has got up and shut the door, and you begin to stand outside and to knock at the door, saying, 'Lord, open to us.'" He will answer you, "I do not know where you come from" (Lk 13:25). Here is a cautionary word. May we not miss the present opportunity, to not wait too long and expect a last-minute rescue: that is simply tempting Providence.

Why do so many of us complain about what we *don't* have, about the lack of orientation in our lives, and about the fact that we don't seem to experience a sense of acceptance or "homecoming" in the faith, when we are so doggedly determined to refuse to *ask, seek,* and *knock*? How do we expect acceptance, understanding, or a sense of homecoming unless we can identify a community that *already exists,* and unless the members of that community are themselves willing to answer when we ask, to accompany us when we seek, and to open when we knock? And how will our communities have the courage of their convictions and live as they are called to live, unless they are encouraged by the promise (endorsed by the Divine Passive): "Knock, and *the door will be opened.*" It is God who will open the door. We have Jesus' promise on it.

We need a conversion. Jesus calls us (in fact commands us) but gently: he does not force us. But he is also quite clear: unless we ask, we will not receive; unless we seek, we will not find; unless we knock, the door will remain shut. But that is only half the story: "The one who asks *always* receives; the one who seeks *always* finds; the one who knocks will *always* have the door opened" (Mt 7:8). Do we want to be converted? Do we believe? Do we trust? Have we tried?

∿

Prayer

Folk wisdom tells us: "If one door closes,
another door opens."
God's wisdom tells us
there's more to it than that.

Jesus tells us to look for closed doors,
not to be deterred by doors that are locked.
He says, "Knock" (persistently perhaps).
And he promises to open doors for us.

There's even more to it than that:
He says he knocks on our doors,
the doors of our hearts.
And reminds us to open up to him.

If we hope, believe, and expect
closed doors to open up to us,
surely we will return the favor
and open our own clay-shuttered doors.

Questions

1. Do we knock on other doors, or stand petulantly, expecting them to open?
2. Are we responsive to people who knock on our doors seeking help?
3. What can we learn from the bridesmaids?

Endnotes

1. Roland Murphy, in *The Jerome Biblical Commentary.* Old Tappan, N.J.: Prentice Hall, 1968, p. 509.

12

"LOVE ONE ANOTHER AS I HAVE LOVED YOU"

John 15:12

The famous Beatles famously sang it: "All you need is love….Love is all you need." It's certainly not original but it does ring in the ear. Yet the more you think of it, the more you might agree that either it is exceedingly naive (in which case we can take it very lightly) or it's most profoundly true (in which case we really need to ponder it deeply and respond appropriately).

Christians and other believers might agree that "all you need is love"—provided "love" refers to the deepest wellspring of one's life. Love-the-wellspring, we can perhaps believe, will generate the life-giving waters of nourishment and growth. When Jesus was verbally jousting with the Samaritan woman at the well, he did two almost contradictory things: he asked her to give him water and he promised to give her water (that would "gush up" to eternal life). He was talking of the God-given, God-derived "living water" that would not only feed her soul and spirit but would provide life for others. At first, she thought of "living water" simply as a kind of labor-saving resource—"so that I may never be thirsty or have to keep coming here to draw water" (Jn 4:15). But before long she began to understand that Jesus was offering something far more radical: a life-changing resource.

For believers, "living water" is understood in two senses: it is both something we constantly thirst for and something that assuages our thirst. So we need to be thirsty in the first place, but our refreshment is only temporary: we soon become thirsty again. The "living water" is nothing less than God's own sustaining love in our lives, a love that both satisfies our appetite and puts a sharper edge on it: we are always hungry and thirsty for God and for God's justice. So even if we obtain the living water, we cannot simply gulp it down or save it for ourselves: it demands to be shared. "Living water" is active and abundant, like a flood that overflows and inundates the surrounding terrain. So the living water of God's love must overflow from us until it becomes life-giving for the parched and deprived. Like living water, love must be the wellspring of our lives.

So what the Beatles sang is radically true: "All you need is love." But it must be true love; it must be authentic and not counterfeit. Only then will it be *all we need*. Probably most people today quite seriously want to believe that all you need is love, but many seem perpetually disappointed, disillusioned, and deprived, and as a result they become soured and cynical. They feel they have tried, and either failed, or been duped; so they give up on love. But come what may, we can never give up on love: that would be to give up on God.

Jesus did not simply command his followers to love, whether selfishly, aimlessly, emotionally, superficially, or whimsically: he was much more directive. "Love one another," he said, "as I have loved you." So, "all you need is love" is only true if we are speaking of the genuine article. Only true love sustains, endures, and satisfies. Only true love is authentically redemptive. Anything less simply lacks the capacity to accomplish what true love can do: change the world. But Jesus does not simply speak of love: he also embodies it, teaches it, tests it in others and proves it himself in the fires of his life and suffering and sacrificial death. "All you need is love"—if it looks like his love.

"Love one another *as I have loved you,*" said Jesus. Sadly, many of us put extremely narrow limits around that "one another," and virtually overlook the "as I have loved you." Yes, we love our own (family, friends, or neighbors), but not uniformly and certainly not unilaterally. Yes, we love our own (by race, religion, or class), but not universally and certainly not unequivocally. So if we want to be disciples and if we want to be obedient to the commandments of Jesus, we will need to remind ourselves that Jesus made a preferential option for the "other"—the socially insignificant (and unloved)—and that he simultaneously called the socially significant (and loved) to change, repentance, and commitment. That is how Jesus loved.

To anyone who received Jesus, by accepting his challenge and invitation, he "gave power to become children of God" (Jn 1:12). What he meant by "receiving" him was becoming a believer: believing him, accepting his teaching, and following his example by observing his commandments. And of all these numerous and varied commandments, the most fundamental—and the one from which all the others flow and to which they all return—is that his followers should love: inclusively, without discrimination, and without limit, *as he loved.* For all our posing and posturing, for all our airy pretension and even our good intentions, we simply do not come close.

Jesus laid down his life for his friends—but he identified his friends inclusively rather than exclusively (Jn 15:14), as *anyone and everyone* who carries out his commands. Going even beyond that, he invoked the simile of the mother hen protecting her brood and the good shepherd ready to die for his flock: these are images of his own loving self. Here is Jesus as God of the Covenant: a God who promises to remain faithful *even if God's people lose faith, become faithless, and break the covenant.* God—in Jesus—will *never* stop loving; he will *never* abandon God's creation. *That* is the measure of the love Jesus has for us. That is the yardstick against which our love will forever fall short.

We sometimes claim to do things "for the love of God," trying to indicate how much we love God and how faithful we try to be. But the First Letter of John famously "deconstructs" this language: "the love of God" refers, first and foremost, to *God's own love:* for us, for others, and for all creation (1 Jn 4:10). So if we want to use that phrase we should remember where it originates and what it implies: the infinite, totally committed, enduring love of God. Not surprisingly, measured in this way, our love appears rather modest.

Thirty years ago, when people were reappropriating the language of love, and using it in socially responsible and theological contexts rather than in a narrowly romantic way, John Powell wrote a popular book, *Why Am I Afraid to Love?* It appealed to people who were finding love to be commitment rather than infatuation. They did not want to give up on the romantic connotations but realized how often selfishness and unrealistic expectations rather than altruism and a spirit of service contaminated relationships and proved to be the kiss of death to a love that had begun with such wide-eyed naivety. So what do we need to know and remember about the love that Jesus requires of us, the love he himself had for those he first commanded to love? "To love another person is to see the face of God" runs a beautiful line from *Les Misérables.* This, surely, is profoundly true for people of faith. To love another person purely is to place one's trust in that person and to be vulnerable to that person. Trust is like a porcelain vase: if it is not received and carefully held, it can fall and shatter; and a shattered vase cannot easily be restored. To be vulnerable is, literally, to be able to be wounded; those who wear a suit of armor attempt to be invulnerable. To be vulnerable is to discard the armor and yet to trust that all will be well. To have one's trust and vulnerability accepted, respected, cherished, and redeemed or vindicated is the rarest of experiences, and surely closer to our understanding of God's embrace than to our common recollection of a human relationship. Trust, vulnerability, and a certain surrender of control characterize interpersonal love.

"Love one another as I have loved you," said Jesus. How much and how often did he trust his disciples? How much did he expose and share his vulnerability, especially with Peter, James, and John in Gethsemane, but also with the Canaanite woman or Martha and Mary? How willing was he to surrender personal control, as when he allowed himself to be invited by Zacchaeus, when he followed the Centurion to his home, or when he went like a lamb to the slaughter. There is no greater love than this, and it expresses itself in trust, in vulnerability, and in surrender.

The love Jesus describes and embodies is a covenantal love. Yet it is not simply a *do ut des,* or a *quid pro quo*—an "I will if you will" kind of covenant. In fact it is almost one-sided: God's love is eternal, never-ending. God's love endures. God's love is not dependent on our return. We see this in Jesus who loved us unto death. We are called—commanded—to manifest this love, this godly love, in our own lives. We are called to love and to make love the center of our lives. This, surely is what Augustine means when he says *Ama, et fac quod vis:* "love–and [then] do what you like."

If we aspire to be faithful to this particular commandment of Jesus, it would surely help if we had some kind of blueprint or template of the kind of love Jesus is speaking of. We have, of course, the whole life and death of Jesus. We also have the reminder that we must love *"in truth and action"* (1 Jn 3:18, italics mine) rather than through easy rhetoric. Then we have that magnificent prayer-poem-hymn from Saint Paul. The First Letter to the Corinthians contains perhaps the most extended and lyrical elaboration of the faces of love. We know it well: too well, perhaps. But if we are called actually to embody love, to be love, *as Jesus was,* then we can perhaps try a useful exercise. Instead of simply saying "love is" all the way through those verses, we might replace the word *love* by our own name, and see how far we get. If we want to claim that we do indeed love one another as Jesus loves us, then we might try to say honestly, "[I am] patient, [I am] kind," and so on. It is unlikely that we will get very far at all, even allowing ourselves the benefit of the doubt; but it may be well worth looking at the challenge. The shallowness of our own claims to love is clearly exposed if we try to continue:

I am not envious or boastful or arrogant or rude. I do not insist on my own way. I am not irritable or resentful. I do not rejoice in wrongdoing but rejoice in the truth. I bear all things, I believe all things, I hope all things, I endure all things.

Impossible though it looks and impossible though it seems when we examine ourselves and even those who love so much more and better than we do, "love one another" remains an imperative, a deeply serious command from Jesus to all who aspire to follow him. And yet we are called to do the impossible, and with God's grace and our own renewed commitment we can come closer to the target. Our example is always Jesus, who loved us to death. He shows us, he encourages us, he empowers us, and then he commands us: "Love one another *as I have loved you.*" The more we remember and value his love for us, the more likely we are to at least try to love one another.

There are times, perhaps many times, in our lives, when love does not seem enough. Sad and sometimes bitter experience tells us that some people are so badly wounded before we reach them that even loving them as much as we can does not seem to help them to love themselves or to be able to live with a degree of happiness. We humans can virtually kill when we refuse to love or when we fail to learn. So sometimes, sadly, our love does not seem to be enough. But still, love is always necessary: Jesus says so. And he commands it, just to underline the point.

The Beatles, too, can take some credit for helping to spread the word: "All you need is love." But there's still so much that they—and we—seem to have overlooked, about what these words really mean, and about how they need to be put into practice and lived.

~

PRAYER

Inexhaustible yet even more thirst-making,
the water you offer is the water that never finally satisfies;
the more we get, the more we need.
Our thirst is never quite assuaged.

And that's the way you want it, Jesus.

Unlimited yet ever more hunger-provoking,
your bread sharpens our hunger, puts an edge on our appetite;
your wine creates ever-deeper desire, never-abating thirst.
Ravenous and parched we are, hungry and thirsty for justice.

And that's the way you want it, Jesus.

If that's good enough for you,
it's good enough for me.
If that's what you want,
I will try to make it what I want, too.

Questions

1. "The Glory of God is [wo]man fully alive" (Saint Ireneus). How alive am I?
2. Do I believe the Beatles? Do I believe Jesus?
3. "Love one another as I have loved you," said Jesus. Am I included in the "you"? Do I believe the love of Jesus active in the *present* moment?

13

"REPENT, AND BELIEVE IN THE GOOD NEWS"

Mark 1:15

It is actually quite difficult *not* to conjure up a mental picture when we see or hear the words of this commandment. Every Hollywood film about Jesus has exploited this dramatic scene in some fashion, whether by focusing on an almost-ranting Jesus, or showing crowds of people dropping everything and rushing pell-mell to gather round him in excited anticipation. We can all fill in the details ourselves.

If it is difficult not to romanticize this historic moment in the Gospel story, it is surely no less difficult to comprehend it and take it to heart here and now in the context of our own lives almost two millennia after Mark captured it in poetic prose. But we must try, for this is not only a commandment of Jesus; it is his very first, and it is clearly addressed to the widest possible audience.

If there is one thing that Mark emphasizes time after time, it is that discipleship is at the core of Jesus' life and ministry. Jesus will articulate, spell out, and be a model of discipleship as he demonstrates his loyal obedience to his *abba*. He will also cast his net as wide as possible to gather as many people as possible: not only men, but women; not only clever or significant people, but the poor and lowly; not only the healthy and self-sufficient, but the sick and needy. It is critically important for Jesus to extend this invitation and to explain what is required:

> Because the Kingdom is now present, it is possible for individuals, through the grace of God, to participate in his reign. But because the Kingdom is now hidden, not here in its eschatological fullness, both repentance and faith are necessary. In spite of the fact that the reign of God has begun, it is still possible for individuals to fail.[1]

Discipleship is for all; it was then, and it remains so now—because now, as then, the kingdom is both "already" and "not yet." Why, then, were so many of us given the idea that Jesus taught a "two-level ethic," with one standard for the elite (clergy, religious) and another for everyone else (ordinary people, laity)?[2] This produced two shocking results: the creation and maintenance of a superior class, and a high degree of codependency by the rest ("ordinary" people or laity, who came to accept that their duty was to pray, pay, and obey). Such a two-tier teaching is a thing of the past, yet its effects have far from disappeared. There are still very many "ordinary" Christians who simply do not realize that they are called—by baptism and confirmation—to real discipleship: discipleship that derives from their taking to heart this fundamental commandment of Jesus. There is also a disturbing *de facto* schism that is breaking up the community, the body of Christ, along the old fault line that separated clergy and laity; but it is a new and deeper fault line now, which is polarizing clergy and laity even more, and threatening to widen indefinitely. This tragedy would not have occurred if everyone had understood that discipleship is for all.

"Repent, and believe in the good news," says Mark's Gospel (1:15); Matthew has Jesus proclaiming, "Repent, for the kingdom of heaven has come near" (Mt 4:17). As we know, the "good news" and the "kingdom of heaven" are intimately related.

Metanoia is the theological synonym for *repentance*. Both Mark

and Matthew use the imperative form here (*metanoeite*). We usually understand this word to mean a change of *heart*, though it
also carries the connotation of moving other parts of our body.[3] A
change of heart can sometimes fail to become a permanent disposition, but Jesus calls people to an entirely new way of life. The two
words, *repent* and *believe*, in this injunction imply a relationship
and not simply an intellectual act. Belief (*pistis*) in this text generally suggests "trust and personal commitment, often with an orientation toward a threatening future."[4] Jesus, then, is making no
distinction between persons, but (implicitly here, though in increasingly more explicit ways) he is calling people to a relationship
with himself—a relationship that will be tested in the fires of social and religious chaos. The contemporary significance for us is
difficult to overlook.

Many reflections on repentance appeal to our sense of guilt
for past trespasses, or perhaps to our sense of outrage at our discovery of what we, or others, have failed to do. Yet, so very often,
despite these appeals, life continues more or less as before. The
best and most challenging reflection on repentance that I know is
in the form of a short reflection in verse. It reads, in part, like this:

Jesus says in his society there is a new way for [people] to
live:

> *You show wisdom, by trusting people;*
> *you handle leadership, by serving;*
> *you handle offenders, by forgiving;*
> *you handle money, by sharing;*
> *you handle enemies, by loving;*
> *and you handle violence, by suffering.*

In fact you have a new attitude toward everything,
toward everybody.
Because this is a Jesus society, and you repent,
not by feeling bad, but by thinking different[ly].[5]

Most of us can surely identify the "feeling bad" syndrome: sometimes, the "badder" we felt, the better we felt! But if Catholics had it down to a fine art, many Lutherans insist that they were often far, far better at feeling bad than we were. We can laugh about it now; but not only is it a bogus form of repentance, but more seriously, it fails to alleviate other people's suffering or dismantle the structures of injustice. Thinking differently—provided, of course, that it leads to acting differently—is a much better test of authentic repentance. But there is a snag.

As we grow up, processes of socialization form us into the mature adults we will become. Socialization in this sense requires a great deal of learning, of trial and error, and of habit-forming and virtue-forming behavior. But the older we get, the more difficult it becomes to change some of our ways of thinking. Such is the efficiency of political, intellectual, or religious socialization that it is quite difficult to think our thought is wrong! So, to repent by thinking differently is a good deal more easily said than done; it's much easier to feel bad (and do nothing)! If the biblical idea of repentance implies a radical reorientation, then it really presupposes and requires a modification in fundamental ways of thinking lest it fail to be as profound as it needs to be. Saying "Lord, Lord" is no sure sign of repentance; only those who do the will of God will make the grade. But *how* will we change our thinking?

In the history of Christian thought, repentance has been identified by its fruits. Contrition, confession, and satisfaction are the components most familiar to generations of believers. Satisfaction includes restitution where possible, as well as a firm purpose of amendment: a commitment to amend one's life. This does indeed require that we think and act differently, and not just once. The Latin word for repentance (*penitentia*) gives us the notion of "penance," which is itself a form of restitution. But the heart of repentance is a (re)turn to God; and authentic repentance should spring from one's own love for God. This, of course, takes us back to the critically important notion—mentioned several times in these pages—of a relationship with God. This is exactly what Jesus implies as underlying his command to "repent, and believe." But any authentic, developing relationship builds on our willingness to think and act differently; otherwise we are neither responsive nor attentive to the changing reality of every day.

It would be very dangerous if we were to imagine that Jesus is calling us to believe "in the good news" as if that were like believing something we have been told (like an article in a newspaper or an argument in a book). We need to remember that in a very real sense, Jesus *is* the Good News. He is the *incarnation of God's word*, God's message—a message of life and a life-giving message. *Evangelization*, the word we derive from the Greek for good news, is a verb form: it would be equivalent to "good newsing" if we had such a verb. It refers to something very dynamic (not at all like yesterday's news or yesterday's newspaper). Jesus' whole life is spent in good newsing, in being good news.

Jesus is not telling people about something taking place elsewhere; he is drawing them to himself as the good news; he is telling them about himself, his purpose, his own *raison d'être*. When he calls people to repent and believe in the good news, Jesus is calling them to believe *him*, and to believe *in him*, personally. Faith is not simply attached to what Jesus says (the good news) in isolation from him: faith is an attachment and a commitment to the one who both proclaims the life-giving message and leads the way to the kingdom of heaven. Discipleship is simply the following of Jesus who identifies the in-breaking of the kingdom and leads to its fullness. So Matthew's "repent, for the kingdom of heaven has come near" is a virtual paraphrase of Mark's "repent, and believe in the good news." Repentance in this mode, with the modifications it requires in the lives of those who want to repent, produces conversion: the fruit of authentic discipleship.

Conversion requires a *beginning*. It is not only a matter of gritting one's teeth, going through the motions, and enduring to the end; it requires that we begin a life of faith, a life that intersects with the life and person of Jesus Christ. Jewish writer Elie Wiesel added a further dimension, though he was not looking specifically at Christian conversion. He said that God, who is the only one with power to begin anything, has given us a share in that power. By God's grace, therefore, not only can we begin, *we can begin again and again.* This surely touches the core of conversion itself: we can, and we must, see conversion as a continuous and lifelong process of turning, and turning again (as a huge airliner or gigantic oil tanker turns by stages until it is aligned with the runway or harbor entrance), of repenting over and over, of thinking and acting in increasingly godly ways, and of choosing life each day rather than becoming victims or passive recipients.

Dennis Sweetland concludes his study of discipleship in Mark, with a fine reflection on repentance and conversion. Reminding us again that the radical demands of Jesus are not only addressed to the Twelve and their successors (understood as the clergy). On the contrary, because the Twelve are presented as symbolic of all disciples, what is required of them is expected of all. "[Mark's Gospel pictures] an egalitarian community in which all who do the will of God are brothers and sisters of Jesus and in which the Gentile-like exercise of power and authority is prohibited. Mark teaches us that there should be no racial, sexual, economic, or age discrimination in the church."[6] We still have a long way to go, individually and institutionally, before we can persuade ourselves that we have obeyed this command of Jesus to "repent, and believe in the good news."

Mark "calls for all Christians honestly to assess the status of their commitment to the person and work of Jesus. Many who emphasize trust or hope would do well to consider Mark's emphasis on doing, not just hearing, the word of God. Others who have turned discipleship into a kind of legalism, emphasizing obedience above all else, would do well to consider the Gospel's emphasis on 'believing,' on trust and on hope."[7] It important that we strive for such a balance: not the balance that suits us, but the balance that Jesus asks. The repentance Jesus wants from us (and it *is, truly,* for our own good) must touch and affect the whole of life: it must send us out in mission; it must reshape our ethics and fashion our integrity; and it must suffuse all our relationships and sustain our communities.

The depth of our ongoing conversion can be measured by our obedience to, and trust in, Jesus. The quality of our repentance can be gauged by our detachment from wealth and possessions, our hunger and thirst for justice, and a foundational commitment to peace. "Jesus, the Suffering Servant, has given us an example to follow. We must take up our cross and follow him, ready to lose our life if necessary, in the nonviolent service of the Gospel. In both word and deed, Jesus tells us that discipleship means to serve, not to be served."[8] There is no other way: we must repent, and believe in the Good News.

~

Prayer

How long, Lord, before I let go?
How long, Lord, before I catch on?
I want to cling to my own big ideas,
so I don't have a free
hand for yours.

If I really want to catch on and repent,
I need to relax, let go, and think differently.

You promise to be there; to catch me if I fall.
You never break your promises; you always break my fall.

How long, Lord? How long till I really believe the good news?

Questions

1. Is my belief focused on Jesus, or on statements or propositions?
2. Dare I let go of some propositions in order to cling to the person of Jesus?
3. Paul said, "I know in whom I have believed" (2 Tim 1:12). Do I?

Endnotes

1. Dennis Sweetland, *Our Journey With Jesus: Discipleship According to Mark.* Wilmington, Dela.: Michael Glazier, 1987, 162.
2. Much of this section is taken from Sweetland's conclusion: 162–69.
3. In the Chapter "Go Home to Your People and Tell Them," we considered the Hebrew word *shub*, whose root means "to return home" but under God's influence rather than on our initiative.
4. John Donahue and Daniel Harrington, *The Gospel of Mark.* Collegeville, Minn.: Michael Glazier/Liturgical Press, 2002, 71.
5. Rudy Wiebe, *The Blue Mountains of China.* McClelland and Stewart, Toronto, 1970, 1970, 215–6.
6. Sweetland, 164–5.
7. Sweetland, 175.
8. Sweetland, 169.

14

"SEEK, AND YOU WILL FIND"

Matthew 7:7

Growing up in England, we kids used to play a game called "How Green You Are." It goes by different names, but is very similar wherever it is found. While the child who is "it" remains outside the room, a parent or someone inside the room hides an object. Then "it" is invited back into the room to find the hidden object in the quickest time possible—but *not* by searching in the conventional way. As "it" moves across the room, everyone begins singing, "How green you are, how green you are, how green you are, how green you are, how green"—more loudly when "it" approaches the hidden object, and more quietly when "it" moves farther away. A clever, or lucky, child will soon find the object.

Whenever I was "it," I always had a mixed reaction: if the singing immediately grew louder, I was encouraged to continue the search; if *diminuendo* followed *crescendo,* I became frustrated, and then very quickly embarrassed. This unpredictable game could be exiting or acutely uncomfortable; seeking was enjoyable if the rewards were immediate. Otherwise it became burdensome and even painful. Jesus said that one of the prime reasons he had come was to seek. He came to seek the lost, and though he found some of them quickly, at other times the experience was rather more difficult, if not painful. Originally, he identified the lost only as the "lost sheep of the house of Israel" (Mt 15:24), until the Canaanite woman challenged him to widen his own search. (In fact, she is also an excellent example of someone who *asked* and *received.*) She even seems to have caught Jesus off guard and taken him by surprise! Nevertheless, he affirmed her intuitions by exclaiming, "Woman, great is your faith!" (Mt 15:28); and he promised that she would receive what she was asking for.

Jesus then (gradually) came to know who and what he was looking for, even if not everyone else did. He knew who was lost in all kinds of ways, and he tried to help them all, even those who insisted that they were not lost! But the ministry of Jesus was not limited to seeking out the lost; he also encouraged others, and specifically his would-be disciples, to seek for themselves. He did not want people to wander aimlessly through life, nor merely huddle or curl up and wait (like lost sheep perhaps) until they were found (but he also said he had come even for such as they). Nevertheless, he expected people to have a certain sense of direction, a degree of purpose, a measure of resourcefulness.[1]

What exactly did Jesus command them to seek; and where; and how? The whole of his life was dedicated to helping people see more clearly, and hear more acutely, and make decisions more responsibly. He had no intention of depriving them of their self-respect or their basic responsibilities. On the contrary, he insisted that they take responsibility for their own actions and for the lives of each other. Almost immediately after the injunction to seek (Mt 7:7), Jesus says: "Thus you will know them by their fruits. 'Not everyone who says to me "Lord, Lord," will enter the kingdom of heaven, but only the one who does the will of my Father in heaven'" (Mt 7:20–21). Jesus then was not remotely interested in "brainwashing" or acting like a cult leader; people were to be invited to choose and to seek freely. And yet Jesus was also at pains to give them something worth choosing, something worth

seeking; without a certain variety or freedom there is no honest
choosing.

So it is that when Jesus tells people—urges them, commands
them—to seek, he also orients them in a certain direction, warning them to "enter through the narrow gate" (Mt 7:13), to "beware
of false prophets" (Mt 7:15) or to beware of the "yeast of the Pharisees" (Mt 16:11)—those "hypocrites" who put on a show as one
might put on a mask, those "whitened sepulchers" that look so
well cared for and perfectly aligned but are nothing but a sham
cover for desiccated bones and disarticulated skeletons (Mt 23:27–
28). Jesus cautions, advises, and counsels people to obey the law
but not to imitate the lawgivers, to trust in God, and above all to
look to him as model and guide. In other words, Jesus frequently
and in considerable detail shows people exactly what they should
be seeking and where they should look. If we, today, want to carry
out this command, we need to remember that the search first applies to the kingdom, the realm, the will of God. Jesus introduced
the commands to ask, seek, and knock by telling people exactly
what was involved: they should *seek first* God's kingdom and God's
righteousness, and everything else would be theirs as well (Mt 6:33).

To make it even clearer, Jesus declares that, although that realm
is "not yet," it is indeed "already"; it is visible all around, wherever
God's will is being done, wherever people love their neighbor as
themselves, and wherever they neither fight nor retaliate. The realm
is found where two or three are gathered in faith, where forgiveness is a present reality, where gender or ethnicity or social status
confer no privileges and are no indicators of moral worth (Gal
3:28), and where brothers and sisters are committed to searching
and seeking the pearl of great price or the treasure hidden in a
field. Anyone who followed Jesus from town to town, and anyone
who heard the gossip from those who did—in other words, anyone who had ears to hear, and listened carefully—would have been
quite clear about how, where, and for what they should seek. If we
ourselves still don't know, then we simply haven't been looking, or
listening, or trying hard enough to follow. If we find ourselves

wandering rather aimlessly through life, lacking a sense of direction, or without purpose, it may be time for us to think about how we might reorient our lives.

The Gilbert Islands in the Central Pacific have been familiar to generations of philatelists. Now known as Kiribati (a phonetic spelling of the way the local people used to pronounce "Gilberts," and pronounced KIRI-BASS), they became world famous on January 1, 2000 (the birthday of the new millennium), when television pictures of that first sunrise were beamed across the face of the earth. But long before stamps and long before a new millennium, the Gilbertese people had an unequaled reputation as mariners. Without sextant or compass, they could sail their long, ocean-going canoes for sixty or even eighty days across the trackless seas— and find a spit or speck of land only meters above the waves and as little as a quarter of a mile across. How did they accomplish such astonishing feats, time and time again, never in the same weather and rarely in the same direction, but always intentionally, always with a true sense of direction?

"Seek," said Jesus. The mariners of Kiribati seek the most elusive and difficult-to-find landfalls. But to be able to navigate those canoes at all is the work of a lifetime. The community will select a boy, perhaps as young as seven or eight, as a potential navigator. But that is only the very beginning. He will take his place in a canoe, alongside an older, wiser man who will be his mentor in the art of navigation. He will watch, and learn, and ask. Perhaps he will not have what it takes, in which case he will not go far. Perhaps he shows true potential, in which case he must prove his developing skill, but also his virtue, for if ever he is given charge of a canoe he will also be given charge of lives, many lives. If all continues well, the prospective mariner will first become a man, and then a senior man, long before he has charge of canoe and crew. And when, finally, he is old enough to die, he is also old enough to sail under the night sky and steer by the stars. He will seek his final destination on a far-off shore, but he will have accumulated the wisdom of centuries and of other mariners, as well as his own rich experience: these will guide him. He is seeking what he has spent a lifetime preparing to find.

We Christians, too, have access to the accumulated wisdom of centuries and of saints, of women and men who have gone before us, marked with the sign of faith. We are called to seek, but not aimlessly; others have sought before us, and others have found. It is for us to learn and to be taught the art of discipleship, so as to be able to follow the stars and to find The Way.

But to be able to find, we must first be willing to search or to seek. If we simply remain exactly where we are and expect things to happen, or if we steadfastly refuse to look, then we will never find anything worthwhile, and we will be wasting our God-given intelligence. People who deny they have lost something—or will not admit that they are lost themselves—simply become more and more frustrated, because every fiber of their being is straining to discover or recover what they will not even admit to having mislaid! To be able to seek in the first place requires honesty: the acknowledgment that something is missing or lost. Those unaware or unwilling cannot possibly undertake a search.

The search or the seeking that Jesus commands is rather focused. It is not a solitary pursuit but needs to be the work of several people, whether friends or community. If we first ask for help (since Jesus also said, "ask") and then mount the search, then whoever responds to our initial request for help will also accompany us and assist us in our search. So, not only must we be willing to seek, we must be willing to *ask* for assistance! Those who insist on doing everything for themselves will not be inclined to acknowledge other people's help; but without such help they will never find. The search to which disciples of Jesus are committed takes place in groups, in communities. This becomes clearer when we listen to what Jesus promises later, after he has issued his commands.

To be able to find, we must be willing to seek. That itself is an acknowledgment of our incompleteness; we do not already have what we seek, or want, or need. Some people have been brought up never to ask and not to need: either to be self-sufficient ("Neither a borrower nor a lender be"; "owe no one anything" [a misquotation from Romans 13:8]) or to be acquiescent or passive. There is some virtue in thrift, in saving, and in being satisfied with what we have. But there may also be some vice: a certain pride or unwillingness to stir ourselves and go in search of something we truly lack and truly need. As this most often requires us to engage others, we would also be required to acknowledge our need and allow ourselves to be vulnerable. Vulnerable people can be hurt. Vulnerable people can also be helped if others are aware of their need. Christian disciples will allow themselves to be vulnerable, will even risk being hurt, but will always allow themselves to be helped. When Jesus commands us to seek and search, he also promises that our efforts will not be in vain; we will be given the necessary help, and we will, in fact, find. According to Jesus, "The one who seeks *always* finds" (see Mt 7:8). Do we believe? Do we trust? Have we tried?

When Jesus talks about seeking, in the context of the kingdom, strictly speaking, the focal point is the pearl rather than the pearl-fisher, the treasure rather than the treasure-seeker (Mt 13:44–46). But both the pearl-fisher and the treasure-seeker are necessary if the kingdom is to be found, appropriated, and experienced. After all, Jesus is not telling us about an unattainable kingdom, but about one that is already breaking through into the world, a realm into which everyone is invited. He is urging people to seek it with the passion of the pearl-fisher or the treasure-seeker. Such people need a sense of purpose and an enthusiastic commitment, as well as a certain intuition. The pearl-fisher may not yet have found the pearl of great price, nor may the treasure-seeker have unearthed the ultimate treasure: nevertheless they are committed to the search—and they will surely recognize what they are seeking when they find it! And find it they will. We have the word of Jesus on it!

Jesus commands that we ask, although he does so by way of an invitation. But more than that: he underwrites the command with a full guarantee that whoever asks will receive. What could be more inviting than that!

~

Prayer

"Seek," said Jesus. "And you will find"—
but not aimlessly, and not just anywhere.
You must know when and where to look;
and you must seek life.

On Easter morning, women reached the tomb,
and two strange men had news for them:
"Do not seek the living among the dead.
He is not here, but has risen."

So let's be careful and let's be clear:
Seek, we must but life is what we seek.
Jesus is Way and Truth and Life.
Our life's work is to seek Life.

Questions

1. Have I a sense of adventure, a spirit of seeking, like the Gilbertese?
2. Do I reflect adequately on where my search is taking me?
3. Am I at peace—and yet still somewhat restless in my pursuit of God?

Endnotes

1. This raises a question not pursued here: the relationship between the "vertical" and the "horizontal" dimensions of discipleship. Some have maintained that Jesus is calling people only to an intimate and private relationship with God ("verti-

cal"). Others insist on the importance of coming to Jesus *and* being sent to others. This is the "horizontal" dimension of discipleship. It is also the social, or community, dimension. See Dennis M. Sweetland, *Our Journey With Jesus: Discipleship According to Mark.* Wilmington, Dela.: Michael Glazier, 1987, 85–105. I find myself solidly among the "others."

15

"Take Nothing for Your Journey"

Luke 9:3

Mark's account is the oldest of our Gospels. There, Jesus calls the Twelve, sends them out in pairs, and charges them to take nothing for the journey—except a staff (Mk 6:8). But this narrative is in indirect speech: Mark does not put actual words on Jesus' lips. Later, Matthew uses Mark's account, but adds the word *disciples* to the phrase "the twelve," and has Jesus actually say, "Take… no bag for your journey" (Mt 10:1, 9–10). Then in Luke's account (and Luke is the evangelist who best elaborates the *missionary* or centrifugal dimension of the Gospel), there is a very deliberate sequence in which Jesus *calls* the Twelve, *empowers* them, and *sends* them out to *proclaim* the kingdom and to *heal*. Though, unlike Matthew, he does not use the more inclusive word *disciple*, I want to use Luke's account of the commandment under review here, and suggest that it has a radical and universal component that applies to everyone who wants to be considered a disciple of Jesus.

Luke's narrative uses direct speech, then, and Jesus says: "Take nothing for your journey, no staff, nor bag, nor bread, nor money— not even an extra tunic" (Lk 9:3). This is one of the most radical and explicit of all the Gospel sayings and, precisely because of that, it is perhaps tempting for some of us to claim exemption: we are *not* "the Twelve," so this radical command cannot apply to us! But it is surely worth pondering. We might even discover a challenge that might make a difference in our lives and the lives of others.

You may have noticed that Mark's text says the disciples should take nothing *except a staff,* while Luke's says they should take nothing, *absolutely nothing,* and identifies all the things that should *not* accompany them. Without getting caught up in exegesis and the social setting of different Gospel accounts, here are a few remarks. A staff was the emblem of a member of a particular group of itinerant preachers around the time of Jesus,[1] and readers or those who heard this Gospel account would have known that. Mark may have been showing his approval of such people, and encouraging his own community to identify their discipleship by this means. But a staff can also serve as a weapon.

What if Luke is calling for an entirely new expression of godliness, something quite original in the preaching of Jesus; something with no precedent; something that made no place for weapons? We might also remember the place of *hyperbole*: the text does not offer cheap discipleship, but paints an extreme picture. Hyperbole may have its place here, but it does not give us license to take the saying lightly, much less to avoid considering it carefully.

I recall a homily by a member of my own religious community[2] who observed that in biblical times, going into the Temple required that *everything be left behind.* In itself, this is an unexceptionable point. But he then suggested that for Christians the whole world is now like the Temple: focal point, sacred space, and dwelling place of God. The actual Temple no longer exists, but God has not forsaken this people or the world God created. It is the stipulation that *everything be left behind* that is so pertinent here. One of the most obvious reasons for going up to the Temple empty-handed would be to acknowledge that one cannot add anything to God, or that standing figuratively naked before God shows respect for God's sovereignty, acknowledgment of one's own dependence, and modest anticipation of God's blessing. These are dispositions and qualities we might ponder as we return to Luke's text.

"Take nothing for your journey." So a journey is involved here: Jesus is *sending* people. And he is sending them *to other people*. Indeed, this is the whole point: Jesus is commissioning disciples and sending them as delegates of the good news. The force of the actual command "Take nothing for your journey, no staff, nor bag, nor bread, nor money—not even an extra tunic" is a function of the concrete circumstances in which it will be carried out. Who would set out without a staff (the sign of an itinerant preacher)—except someone willing to forego even that tiny mark of identification and perhaps of status? Who would intentionally travel without a bag, or bread—other than someone in a great hurry, or someone whose journey was short, or someone who expected to be received civilly by others? Who, if not someone irresponsible, would travel without money—apart from someone willing to take risks and not wanting to be entirely independent or self-contained? And who would begin a journey with no clear destination and yet fail to take an extra tunic—except a very foolish or very trusting person?

As we look more closely at the full significance of this complex commandment, we may well reflect on the "baggage" that has become a virtual necessity in our own lives. "Don't leave home without it!" a well-known advertisement reminds us. We live in a world that constantly tells us we *absolutely need* this, we *can't possibly manage* without that, and we are *nobody* unless we acquire the other. We are surrounded, encumbered, weighed down by the paraphernalia and impedimenta[3] of life. But when Jesus sends his trusted emissaries to continue his own mission, he tells them: "Take nothing for the journey." We may not be able to take him literally, nor may we be expected to; but we cannot simply turn away and carry on with our own baggage-strewn existence. Even if we were not committed to following Jesus, there are many practical reasons for trying to simplify our complicated lives. We need to stop, to consider what we are doing with our days; as disciples we need to think of the possible *social* significance of our going empty-handed; and, finally and most importantly, we need to enquire what Jesus might be asking of us now.

What are we doing with the days of our lives? Western, consumer capitalist society (and that identifies or includes more of us than we care to admit) is utterly dependent on manufacture and on new technology. Such is the pervasiveness of in-built obsolescence, that not only do people feel pressured to upgrade or replace many of the gadgets or machines on which they depend, but they find themselves caught up in a rabidly competitive culture: they need to have *more*, or *better*, or *different* than other people. Among the various consequences of this is the simple fact that, once seduced by such a culture, there is virtually no escape. The only alternative is to make a consciously countercultural choice: to choose to simplify. Sadly, the problem is compounded by another component of this culture: its emphasis on not being dependent on others or beholden to them. Rural folk still borrow and lend without embarrassment and to mutual benefit, but urban folk tend to live more isolated, private lives. They feel they must satisfy all their needs by acquisition rather than by sharing. Even (particularly?) our religious congregations and orders are not unaffected by this virus: in the name of poverty they have everything they need, and then they invoke prudence ("just in case"), or economy ("we save by bulk-buying") as a justification for certain behaviors! The words of Jesus strike at the very heart of such a mentality.

A second consideration is the possible social significance of willingness to "take nothing for your journey." To feel the full impact of this calls for our imagination: first, we need to imagine the original social context for this commandment, and then we might engage the active imagination by pursuing the twin questions: "what if?" and "why not?"

Jesus lived in a world in which honor was the primary measure of a person's social worth. To gain or accrue honor was life's main task, while to lose it was to be shamed: shame was the very opposite of social capital. It represented not only social bankruptcy but destitution. Complicating the matter was the fact that social and moral worth were virtually inseparable. To be socially significant was to be perceived as a person of moral worth, while to lose social capital was to be perceived as morally destitute as well. As in our own day, cultural values exercised a strong force over a person's life: to survive meant to compete; not to compete was to become socially dead.

A fundamental virtue in Jesus' society, and one practiced just as keenly in the surrounding Greek world, was hospitality. The Greeks said that Zeus, father of the gods, wandered the earth as a stranger. Therefore one must always give preferential service to every stranger in case this particular one was Zeus in disguise. The Jews had a similar notion: not only was their law very explicit about hospitality (Ex 12:48–49; 22:21; 23:9), but they had the example of Abraham. It was said that the longest verse in the Bible is found *between* the first and second verses of Genesis 18. Here it is: (1) *The LORD appeared to Abraham by the oaks of Mamre, as he sat at the entrance of his tent in the heat of the day.* (2) *He looked up and saw three men standing near him.* The transition from "The Lord appeared" to "he...saw three men" is as dramatic as it is significant: the Lord appears *as* three men. Abraham's response was to offer hospitality as sacred duty and godly act. As a result, Sarah was promised a son in her old age.

This topic is immensely rich and complex, but the point, applied to the commandment of Jesus, is quite simple: those who "take nothing for the journey" will not only quickly encounter other people, but can expect to be offered hospitality.[4] There are further implications: in Jesus' society, telling people to take nothing for the journey would certainly have been a challenge, but it was not at all tantamount to sending them to their death. It was, however, asking them to risk trusting people they did not know, to court potential hostility, and to be initially dependent on others.

An interesting aspect of hospitality is this: though it may be a binding obligation, it is not completely open-ended. People need to protect themselves, and those with limited resources cannot be so liberal as to jeopardize their own livelihood (even though they may be amazingly generous *in the short term*). People who seek hospitality will be quite aware of the rules: they must show respect and deference; they must be grateful for what they receive and what the hosts can spare; and they must not tarry. Strangers who are treated like guests must either move on very soon or find a way to contribute to the local community.

Applying these conventions and expectations to the situation at hand, it is easy to see the best-case and worst-case scenario. At best, those who "take nothing for the journey" will find acceptance and new relationships. They will be able to contribute to the local community in a number of possible ways. And they will be able to share the good news: in this case, by proclaiming the kingdom and healing the people (Lk 9:2). At worst, they would be shunned or chased out of town (or even killed). But in a culture of hospitality, to take nothing for the journey is not altogether counterintuitive.

Without a staff as a potential weapon, and lacking even a cloak within which to conceal one, the stranger would not have appeared in an aggressive mode; having neither bag nor bread nor money, he—or, less frequently, she[5]—would clearly be in need. In a culture that prized hospitality, this would invite amity. Local communities would know that the stranger, properly tried and tested, might be someone with whom to bond, to forge new relationships, and from whom to learn news from outside—perhaps even the good news of salvation.

Now each of us can address the final question: what might be Jesus' expectations of us, as we ponder and pray about this command, drawing on our faith and invoking a little imagination?

What if? What if we took risks? What possibilities, what danger, and what opportunities may be opened up? What if we were a little more daring?

Why not? Why not take Jesus more seriously? In a world of clutter and control, of self-sufficiency and self-determination, of competition and confrontation, why not go openhanded and open-minded, on journeys of faith and fellowship?

〜

PRAYER

God of superlatives, God of all,
God of radical goodness!
Because you created us out of love,
you give us all we need.
Because you promised not to abandon us,
you ask for all our trust.

We believe your promises will not be broken,
because you gave us your Word.
Jesus is the word among us, even now—
speaking to us of your faithfulness.

Jesus came with nothing, born poor,
depending on the lowly.
He commissions us to go with nothing,
trusting in the lowly.
He promises to be with us,
dwelling among the lowly.

What if we trusted more?
Why not?

Questions

1. Encumbrances weight us down, but disciples must travel light. Should I make some changes?
2. Can I identify the baggage in my life? Can I leave one single piece behind?
3. "Take nothing for your journey," says Jesus. Can I ponder this today?

Endnotes

1. J. D. Crossan, *The Birth of Christianity*. HarperSanFrancisco, 1998, 278–82. Crossan endorses Horsley's criticism of Gert Theissen, saying, "There is simply no justification in the sources for Theissen's writing…as if the Jesus movement consisted primarily of wandering charismatics," or that "the wandering charismatics are the key to understanding the Jesus movement." Then, departing from Horsley, Crossan makes an important distinction: "There is…a clear difference between the symbolic attire of the Cynic itinerants and that of the kingdom of itinerants. For the former, taking a knapsack and staff indicated personal self-sufficiency. For the latter, *not* taking a knapsack indicated communal dependency" (280). This, I think, is a very telling point.

2. Terence Cascy, CSSp, would be delighted to know his words were remembered!

3. A curiosity: *paraphernalia,* in Roman law, were those small, petty, personal things a bride brought to her husband's house. They were regarded as sentimental and trivial. Perhaps for that reason, she was allowed to retain them as her property. *Impedimenta* referred originally to those things carried by a soldier on a route-march.

4. Another command, which includes the phrase, "shake the dust off your feet," must be understood in the same context as this. It addresses an extreme situation where hospitality is *not* forthcoming, and it suggests a modification or exception to the commandment considered here.

5. Though we should be aware that when Jesus sent his disciples out in pairs, husband and wife teams may have been included: there are compelling reasons to include women among those designated "disciples."

16

"TEAR [YOUR EYE] OUT AND THROW IT AWAY"

Matthew 5:29; 18:9

W hat a violent image and what a self-destructive notion this is! Its vividness is almost nauseating! So what on earth are we to make of it, and how can it possibly stand alongside the other commandments of Jesus—those that seem so much more reasonable, or at least make better sense?

There is a tendency for people to assume that what is not literally true is not true at all, or that what does not make sense literally, must therefore be nonsense. For such people, this commandment will be rejected out of hand because it could not possibly be intended literally; or could it?

Hyperbole is a figure of speech or a rhetorical device that makes a point very effectively by virtue of judicious exaggeration. Such speech is not intended to be taken literally, but it is not *mere* exaggeration either: it serves a purpose in the particular context. When Jesus issues this particular command, he is speaking very, very seriously about the new standard (his proclamation) being higher than the old (the traditional understanding, imperceptibly modified over the centuries). Specifically, at this point, he is talking about adultery. As he proclaims the kingdom, the realm, of God, Jesus calls his hearers to new levels of commitment. He is looking for disciples, people who will take him seriously, glimpse his vision, and work with him to change the world. The instructions and commands he issues are a direct challenge, particularly to people with vested interests, people who do not want to change the world: they like things just as they are. So some people find Jesus, and what he stands for, quite offensive: even scandalous. But Jesus insists both on proclaiming something that strikes his listeners' ears as new, and on inviting people, calling them, to a new way of living. As he does so, he will remind them what scandal really means, why it is so deadly, and why his fledgling community must avoid it at all costs.

By means of hyperbole, Jesus makes a startling contrast between someone lacking an eye because of a self-inflicted act and someone with two perfectly functioning eyes. But *his* point is that the former rather than the latter may actually be more healthy! This is certain to get the crowd's attention.

Jesus is talking about the realm of God, and making the point that before anyone can enter the kingdom of heaven there may well come a moment of truth, a moment of choice. At that moment, he says, the kingdom, or realm, must be given absolute priority: *nothing* is more important. By challenging people even to imagine plucking or tearing out an eye, Jesus is leaving no doubt in their minds about the seriousness of his case. No wonder some people will be angered and offended, and some may turn away in disgust: but no one will be unclear about what Jesus is proposing. Far from commanding people to blind themselves (or to cut off a hand or foot [Mt 18:8]), Jesus is saying precisely the opposite: he is calling them to be so committed to the kingdom that such mutilation would be as unnecessary as it is unthinkable. His hearers would know this: hyperbole is part of every oral culture.

Hyperbole exercises a powerful hold on the imagination. But many contemporary people (perhaps especially those who have been taught to read the Gospel rather literally) fail to appreciate hyperbole. Some simply cannot see when it is being used, and others

have very little imagination. Such people are left to their own devices, caught between the stark words and images of Jesus and their
own intuitions or common sense. Because they cannot accept that
Jesus—in this case at least—could possibly be serious, they simply
move on.

Yet many commandments of Jesus cannot be reduced to the
literal. "Go the extra mile," "turn the other cheek," forgive seventy
times seven": these are not to be understood literally but to be in-
ternalized so deeply that they allow of no escape, no possibility of
self-justification. They do not prescribe and limit, but rather they
amaze us by their open-endedness. Far from putting limits, Jesus
is asking everything, just as, far from offering tangible rewards, he
is offering everything. We must not settle for the possible simply
because we cannot achieve the impossible; we are called, challenged,
and commissioned to *attempt* the impossible. That is the nature of
discipleship. That is why the call and commandments of Jesus are
so compelling and exciting—to those with imagination, and with
faith.

Many years ago, as a hospital chaplain, I was called to a locked
psychiatric ward. Entering the room, I saw a young man sitting on
the floor, head down. The nurse told him I was there and he slowly
lifted his head. His body was bowed, his face was mutilated, the
skin around his eyes was livid and angry—and his eye sockets were
empty. With panic in his voice, he told me that he had been on the
verge of an adulterous relationship and felt powerless to stop himself. Then he had remembered the command of Jesus. So he tore
out—enucleated—both eyes. He wanted me to reassure him that
he had done the right thing and that God had forgiven him. Now
of course he was in a locked psychiatric ward. (What better place
for such a deranged person in our so very rational and civilized
post-Christian world?) The next half hour was one of the most
difficult of my life, and indeed of his. He needed to be understood
and consoled, yet the deed was done, his sight was lost, and he
thought this was what God wanted. Was it? Is this what God asks:
not "an eye for an eye" but an eye for an adulterous thought?

It's important that we stay with this image and try to understand its implications. Jesus was making a comparison: "It were better if something terrible happened than that something even more terrible should happen," or "You must at all costs cling to what is best, even if you should lose what is good." The emphasis is firmly on the extreme, whether positive ("heaven") or negative ("hell"). This produces the dramatic effect (a gasp of shock from the audience). Jesus is saying something like this: "The kingdom is open to all and everyone who chooses it, but you cannot have it both ways: you cannot choose both the kingdom and serious sin." In fact he is even more explicit. He makes the startling assertion that the physical act of adultery is not the only thing to avoid: a deliberate desire and intention to commit the sin is no less sinful.

Adultery is so destructive of persons, families, and of society itself, that even to plan it[1] is enough to be morally guilty: and adulterers will be excluded from the kingdom of God. *Therefore,* says Jesus, whatever you do, make sure that you are not excluded. And if some thing or some person were ever likely to lead you to adultery (your eye, for example), then do whatever it takes, but at all costs avoid the sin. The good must be chosen and the sin must be repudiated, because everything is at stake here. And to emphasize what the "everything" is—eternal life, heaven, the kingdom—Jesus hyperbolically elaborates the comparison: better to chop yourself into pieces, to dismember yourself, in order to ensure your integrity, your wholeness, and your being re-membered in the kingdom of heaven. Of course it should not come to this, but if it did…. Jesus leaves no room for doubt about the most important thing in life.

In his famous interview for *Playboy,* Jimmy Carter admitted (as did Pope John Paul II, though not in the same publication) that he had been tempted to sexual sin. He was making the point that being a Christian is not easy and no guarantee of a "free ride." He was widely ridiculed by members of the *Playboy* culture, which is hardly surprising. What is significant, though, is that the president of the United States took this particular commandment of

Jesus very, very seriously. He was trying to be a disciple. He was implying that he had made a choice, a choice against adultery.

The man I met in the locked psychiatric ward also made a choice. It may have been misguided. It was certainly extreme. But he definitely believed there was something even worse than losing one's sight.

Physical integrity is not the yardstick of moral integrity, and disfigurement is not the hallmark of sinfulness. Jesus spent his entire ministry healing sick people and showing that physical impairment is not the mark of God's disapproval. But nor are physical beauty or prowess sure indications of Divine favor. Jesus spent his entire ministry warning the complacent to look deeply into their souls.

When Jesus issues the commandment to tear out one's eye, he prefaces it, critically, with the conditional, "if." He is talking about scandal, and he later repeats the commandment (Mt 18:9) hard on the heels of a chilling warning about scandalizing others, especially the children. So we must ponder the significance of scandal if we are fully to understand the commandment. The eye (or the foot or hand) must not be allowed to scandalize, either oneself or another member of the community or "one of these little ones who believe in me" (Mt 18:6). The Greek uses the phrase *tôn mikrôn*—"the little (micro) ones." It does not specify children, or the poor, but Matthew typically uses this phrase either to refer to the Twelve Apostles or to the members of his own community.

There are six references to *scandal* in Chapter 18. Literally, it means a trap, a snare, or a stumbling block; in a religious context "it refers to temptation to sin or incitement to apostasy."[2] What Jesus seems to be particularly concerned about therefore is the integrity of the community and the protection of its members. *If* one person should compromise either the community or another member, such a person should be in no doubt about the seriousness of that sin: it would exclude this person from the kingdom of heaven, the realm of God. This is why Jesus teaches through hyperbole and uses the most vivid and unforgettable of imagery. Forewarned is forearmed.

What can we conclude? Jesus takes his disciples every bit as seriously as he wants them to take him. He proclaims not only a kingdom but a new kind of community: a community open to all, inclusive of everyone, and offering support and solidarity to its members. The integrity and the mission of the community must not be compromised, and its members must realize that nothing can be allowed to bring scandal and thereby corrupt it. Better a united, focused, and apostolic community of people less than physically perfect than a community of Amazons or Atlases whose members are terminally corrupt, "whited sepulchers."

We know just how painful it can be when we accidentally tear or pierce our skin. We can keenly recall the deep throbbing of toothache or earache. And we know that it is almost impossible to inflict pain upon ourselves deliberately. The very idea of tearing out an eye is almost unimaginable. That is exactly what we need to remember when we hear this disturbing commandment of Jesus. Rather than an eye or a hand or a foot becoming a source of scandal—to ourselves or to others—we should be prepared, in principle, to "tear it out and throw it away." At all costs we must avoid eternal suffering; at all costs we must avoid giving scandal. This dramatic and cautionary image is both a warning and a directive.

The commandments of Jesus are not easy to live up to, but with God's help they are possible to undertake. Those who commit themselves to keeping them will find life. Jesus said his yoke is easy and his burden light. It does not always seem that way, especially to people bent over by the weight and the pain. But we walk by faith and we try to love, however poorly; for we believe that there is virtue in keeping these commandments, and that there is indeed life for those who try and who persevere—even if they end up with sight a little dimmed and hands or feet a little shaky.

∼

Prayer

Lord, you do make life difficult!
You can be so demanding!
It is not surprising you have so few followers.

You tell us to be strong yet to forgive the weak.
You want us to follow, but you expect us to give the lead.
You know we are sinners, but you want us to be perfect.
How can we possibly measure up?

We need to know you better.
We need to find your Way.
We need your strength and courage.
We need to learn to trust.

Lord, our life is not always easy.
You do not even promise to make it so.
But by carrying our burden and sharing our yoke,
you do make it possible, and good.

Questions

1. "Deny yourself," says Jesus. What does this mean to me? Is it hyperbole?
2. "Take up your cross," says Jesus. Is this just a figure of speech?
3. "Follow me," says Jesus. Is this my current intention?

Endnotes

1. Thinking about, even pleasurably, is not the same as planning, which is a good deal more premeditated and detailed.
2. Daniel J. Harrington, *The Gospel of Matthew.* Collegeville, Minn.: Michael Glazier/Liturgical Press, 1991, 264.

17

"TURN THE OTHER CHEEK"

Matthew 5:39

I t all depends on what you mean by…": we have heard these
words so often, from people who need to justify themselves,
from those who want to show how clever they are, or just from
people who are confused. In the case of this particular commandment, we might begin by saying that it does indeed all depend on
what someone (whether it is Jesus, Matthew, Luke, the early Church,
an exegete, or oneself) means by the phrase. The meaning is not
too clear; and it is almost confusing enough to make us leave it
alone or walk away. But of course we can't do that!

We start with two points, both of which may be familiar. First,
we have here another instance of *hyperbole*[1] (not to be confused
with exaggeration, but certainly not giving us license to disregard
or diminish what is being said). Second, if a right-handed person
hits you on your *right* cheek, then you will have felt the *back* of
your assailant's hand; if the blow had been struck with the palm of
the hand, it would have landed on your *left* cheek. Can these points
add to our understanding of the force of Jesus' command that we
turn the other cheek?

Jesus seems to be saying something like this: even if someone has so little respect for you and so much aggression toward you as to add injury to insult by viciously striking you in the face, not only should you not retaliate, you should respond by assuming a stance of such vulnerability that you might even be knocked unconscious by the next, uncontested blow! This is a command of breathtaking directness, and it even smacks of provocation to extreme foolhardiness. What could it possibly lead to?

On the face of it, the act of turning the other cheek is indeed foolish, and deserving of all it gets. If a bully or a thug is the aggressor, nonretaliation may simply provoke him. But perhaps there is some depth psychology at work. Unquestionably, there is risk involved, since we can never predict other people's behavior, much less that of violent and aggressive opponents.

For one person to strike another in the face, there must already have been a highly emotional outburst. Perhaps the aggressor feels deeply aggrieved and is retaliating to some hurt, whether verbal or physical. But these words of Jesus assume that the recipient of the blow is an innocent party. Therefore, the aggressor must have either *felt* slighted or insulted, or must be quite irrationally aggressive. In the former case, there must have been a previous encounter between the two, or an incident to provoke the outburst, or perhaps even a previous relationship that is about to be put to the sternest of tests. In the latter case, one can imagine the recipient of the blow being completely taken aback by the unprovoked aggression. But whatever the circumstances, whatever the justification, whatever the provocation, the command of Jesus remains one and the same: turn the other cheek, do not retaliate, and indeed allow for a possible second strike! It is all rather difficult to understand.

A dear friend works in a home for elderly people. Because of poor pay and poor management, some of the healthcare is atrocious and many patients, incontinent and senile, are neglected and abused. Anyone deeply committed to the patients is equally likely to antagonize the less responsible members of the staff. For my friend, every day is a struggle to turn the other cheek, rather than to retaliate or quit. If she did that, her life would be less stressful but the patients would continue to be without an advocate. Her life is a true witness to the Gospel and a sign of just how demanding this commandment can be.

Jesus surely knows that discipleship entails risk (being what Saint Paul calls a fool for Christ's sake [1 Cor 4:10]); but discipleship is also intended to renew families, communities, and the world. So Jesus is not encouraging masochism. Part of the issue, at least, concerns the aftermath or consequences. What would be the point of turning the other cheek—socially speaking, or from the perspective of the community? The answer seems to be embedded in the broader context of this command.

Biblical theologians would make important distinctions between what Jesus (probably) said, and how the evangelist(s) used his sayings in their own context. This is entirely legitimate, and has produced wonderful insights.[2] It *is* important to distinguish the purposes of Matthew and Luke (in this instance), to contrast the social worlds of the early wandering prophets, the latter settled communities, and the contemporary world(s) of the twenty-first century. Nevertheless, as Gerd Theissen reminds us, "Jesus' demand goes far beyond every specific situation. It is general."[3] It is the universal or all-embracing application of the commandments of Jesus that we try to come to terms with in these pages.

Jesus has been sketching a profile of the disciple: whoever follows him is called to a higher standard than the scribes and Pharisees (Mt 5:20). This is already an enormous challenge, given that Jesus tended to attract what Dominic Crossan calls "a community of nobodies," and that the scribes and Pharisees were perceived as strict religious observers. The passage in which the "turn the other cheek" command is placed is part of the gathering climax of Matthew's chapter that begins with the beatitudes. Jesus has raised the bar several times since beginning his Sermon on the Mount. Moving beyond the familiar "thou shalt not kill," he has called his followers to set a bold example: they must not indulge in destructive anger or demeaning name-calling (Mt 5:21–23). Instead of

seeking legal recourse against another member of the community, the disciple is required to seek reconciliation. Rather than
self-righteously avoiding adultery, the follower of Jesus is called to
self-control and the mastery of lustful longings and desires. It is a
tall order but unequivocally clear: the standards by which "ordinary" people will be judged are not high enough or stringent
enough for disciples of Jesus. This is more than enough to give *us*
pause, and to make us very conscious of our failures.

But Jesus was not finished. To drive the point home, he raised
the standards that will apply to disciples, in respect of marriage
and divorce, oath-taking, and the personal rights covered by *lex
talionis* (the law of re-taliation): there will be no claim of "an eye
for an eye," despite this being the classic and time-honored law of
the Medes and the Persians. Rather, the disciple will neither cling
to nor claim such precedent.

It is at this point (still, technically, part of the Sermon on the
Mount) that Jesus introduces the image of turning the other cheek.
But even that is not the end. He follows it up with three other
images or injunctions: not only surrendering one's cloak, but offering one's tunic as well; not merely going the legally required
mile with one who has authority to demand it, but going an extra
mile as well; and not only giving to those in obvious need, but to
whoever asks for a free gift or seeks to borrow against the promise
of a later return.[4]

As we reflect on the psychology of what Jesus demands of his
followers, it becomes increasingly obvious that they are required
to be vulnerable, to take risks, to gamble with their reputation and
their safety. They are not promised human justice, but challenged
to open themselves to the possibility of exploitation. What could
this mean?

Cultural anthropologist George Foster developed the notion
of "limited good" in the 1960s. This was subsequently embellished
by others and called the "zero-sum" game or strategy. The idea
behind it was that virtue—specifically honor or reputation (and
its cultural companion: shame)—was understood to be something

like a commodity. One person could hold or accrue it, but always at the expense of another, since there was only a "limited" amount, and not enough to go round. Consequently, there would always be competition to acquire it, and concern lest it be lost. But Jesus was at pains to point out the crippling effects of such a view and of the competitive spirit it inevitably engendered. "It must not be like this among you," he would say.

Jesus did not play the zero-sum game. He did not seek to accrue honor like credit in a bank. He was not concerned that his actions might bring shame and diminish his honor. He did not seek to shame others and thereby increase his own honor. On the contrary, he consorted with "shameful" people: tax collectors, sinners, and those considered to be polluted and polluting. Far from avoiding people such as these, he seemed to go out of his way to gather with them, to touch them, to heal them. He rejected the idea that he could be contaminated by their pollution, and seemed determined to practice a "reverse contamination" by contaminating others with his holiness and healing power.

For Jesus, the notion of competition with its inevitable outcome of winners and losers was totally unacceptable: God has no favorites, God's grace is not a limited good, and life is not a zero-sum game. It seems to me that we have to approach the command to turn the other cheek with these points in mind. Jesus was preaching something both new and very challenging. It is suggested that the primary context of this Jesus-saying for Matthew's community was the problem of "enemies" within one's own household, resulting from one's commitment to Jesus. "The Jesus movement was breaking up households. Parents, frustrated [*dishonored*] at being unable verbally to dissuade their children of the folly and *shame* of their new commitment, were driven to 'strike them on the left cheek.'"[5] Jesus encouraged them to turn the *other* cheek. This implied both that they repudiated the prevailing notion of shame, but that they were not afraid to bring shame upon their parents, if that is what discipleship implied. The world was being turned on its head.

In an *agonistic* culture such as that of first-century Palestine, honor was accrued or defended through fighting or contesting. If someone is looking for a fight, he is anticipating being the winner, either by causing his opponent to withdraw (and be shamed thereby), or making a loser out of him (and shaming him anyway). If the would-be opponent retaliates, battle lines are drawn and the drama proceeds until winner and loser are determined. So, what if the would-be opponent fails to retaliate or withdraw, but turns the other cheek? Then a win could only be achieved by bullying or by an unfair fight: that would not bring honor on the aggressor, but shame. But if the would-be aggressor saw that there could be no fair fight, then assuming him to be an honorable man,[6] he would have to disengage and even apologize. Hostilities would cease, and tempers could cool. The implications here, for disciples and for families, are palpable.

Jesus is rejecting the whole agonistic rationale: what matters is not culturally constructed honor and shame, but God's justice and people's faithfulness to God and God's promises. Jesus unmasks the poverty of a religious culture built on honor and shame, and calls his disciples to live by different criteria: love of God and love of neighbor. To turn the other cheek may be to invite gratuitous violence. It is also to create an alternative possibility, the possibility that the aggressor may rethink, and desist. The animal kingdom offers numerous examples of creatures that, when attacked by one of their own kind, actually lie on the ground, on their back, offering no resistance. In many cases, this ritual response serves to defuse the situation and the aggressor walks away. If animals have learned the meaning and potential of metaphorically turning the other cheek, disciples of Jesus can surely do likewise. But it is a monumental challenge. Whenever I am in conversation with my nursing friend, I am reminded of the cost of discipleship, and of the fact that all around, unnoticed and unsung, there are people who practice it on a daily basis.

Finally, and in rather stark contrast, I am reminded of a moment from years ago. A young, recently married Jewish woman was involved in a head-on collision on the interstate near Albany, New York. Her spinal cord was virtually severed, but she had almost no external injuries. Her husband, a neurologist, was in New York City, 150 miles away. By the time he would have arrived, her paralysis would most likely be complete. There being no rabbi available, I was called to her bedside. She was very beautiful and very vulnerable; I was very young and exceedingly self-conscious. She smiled, and without preamble but very respectfully, she asked if she might touch my face. Hardly breathing, but somehow trusting the grace of the moment, I leaned over her bed as she raised her hand and very slowly, with eyes closed, traced every feature of my profile. Then, with great dignity and calm she said that her husband was on his way but would not arrive in time. Mine was quite possibly that last human face she would touch. She wanted to be able to remember it, and she was very grateful to me, she said. I found myself so moved by the moment, that instinctively I turned the other cheek, and she caressed it gently with the back of her hand.

~

PRAYER

Discipleship should not necessarily be easy,
but does it need to be so difficult?
To turn the other cheek
is almost literally impossible?

But if discipleship is a matter of learning,
maybe it is supposed to be progressive.
If it's a matter of following,
maybe it takes a while.

When you called Peter out of the boat,
you called him to do the impossible.
Why should I expect to be a disciple,
unless I'm willing to do the same?

> *Politics is the art of the possible,*
> *But discipleship is much, much more.*
> *For those who walk the Way of Jesus,*
> *God will make miracles happen.*

Questions

1. Do I always need to have the last word?
2. Is vulnerability the same as weakness?
3. Violence breeds violence: can it ever stop?

Endnotes

1. See the previous chapter: "Tear [Your Eye] Out and Throw It Away."
2. See Aaron Milavec, "The Social Setting of 'Turning the Other Cheek' and 'Loving One's Enemies'" in light of the *Didache*. *Biblical Theology Bulletin*, 3, 1995, 131–143; also, *The Didache*. Collegeville, Minn.: The Liturgical Press, 2004.
3. Quoted in Milavec, op. cit., 132; From Theissen, G., "Nonviolence and Love of Our Enemies." *Social Reality and the Early Christians*. Minneapolis, Minn.: Fortress Press, 1992, 115–56.
4. Again, Milavec summarizes very well the varied implications of these injunctions.
5. Milavec, op. cit., 143. My emphasis.
6. Honor was held or lost by men. Women could bring shame to their menfolk, but could not accrue honor.